The London Coffee Guide.
2013

Edited by
Jeffrey Young
and Guy Simpson

Author: Allegra Strategies
Photography: Maximilian Gower,
Joan Torrelles and Warattaya S. Bullôt
Design: John Osborne
Website: Tim Spring and Lee Goldsmith
Other content: Sally Conor
Publisher: Allegra Publications Ltd

Allegra
PUBLICATIONS

Published in 2013 by Allegra Publications Ltd, No.1 Northumberland Ave, Trafalgar Square, London, WC2N 5BW

Visit our website:
www.londoncoffeeguide.com

All information was accurate at time of going to press.

Published by *Allegra* PUBLICATIONS Ltd © 2013

No.1 Northumberland Ave, Trafalgar Square, London, WC2N 5BW

Foreword

by **Stephen Hurst**, Founder/Owner, Mercanta The Coffee Hunters and London School of Coffee, Board of Directors 2004-2010, Alliance for Coffee Excellence

I think it is worth noting, that this guide would have been virtually impossible to compile five short years ago.

Has the London quality coffee scene been transformed? Has it evolved? In truth, London has seen a coffee revolution. Energised by UK wins at the World Barista Championship in 2007 and 2009, and driven by an influx of antipodean coffee aficionados, London now takes its rightful place on the specialty coffee map alongside Melbourne, Seattle, Vancouver, Berlin, Portland, San Francisco and New York. No longer will Londoners have to hear the sad refrain from visitors to the capital that it is impossible to find a decent cup of coffee. Now, in certain districts, customers are spoilt for choice.

I often tell people that Mercanta and London School of Coffee are not so much in the coffee business as in the specialty food and beverage business. This is an important distinction. In a world where teas, whisky, beer, wine, olive oil, and even water are understood as differentiated products with considerable variation in quality, price and provenance, coffee still has a long road to travel to be understood not as a commonplace commodity, but as a unique agricultural beverage. The inherent taste of the coffee itself becomes the talking point.

The London that we viewed when we began in 1996 is unrecognisable from the horizon we see today. Back then, Monmouth Coffee and very few others kept the quality candle burning. Now innovation, quality, professionalism and variety can be found on many street corners and within the pages of this guide.

And the best thing is, this London quality coffee house revolution has only just begun.

Contents

Introduction

Welcome to The London Coffee Guide 2013 – the definitive guide to London's independent coffee venues.

The guide was born out of a quest to find the best and most exciting places to go for coffee in London. Following a boom in new openings over the past three years (since the first edition of our guide), London is now home to a thriving and world class independent coffee scene.

We have compiled The London Coffee Guide 2013 to assist and inform people who are keen to travel across this wonderful city in the hunt for great coffee. For some, coffee itself is the main attraction, for others, it's the buzz of visiting a new and unique coffee shop. Our aim is to encourage fellow coffee lovers to try something different and discover places they otherwise might never have known.

This year we have worked with specialist contributors to put together a coffee knowledge section to help readers learn more about and experiment with the coffee they love.

Allegra Strategies is an established leader in consumer and business intelligence for the coffee industry in the UK and Europe. We have drawn on this research as well as experts in the field to compile this edition. We hope you like it.

About the Guide

Ratings

Every venue featured in The London Coffee Guide has been visited and rated by our expert editorial team. The ratings fall into two distinct categories: Coffee Rating and Overall Rating on a score of 1-5, with 5 being the highest possible score. Customer feedback received via The London Coffee Guide website is also fundamental to the rating process, informing both the venue shortlist and the final scores.

COFFEE 4.75 / 5   OVERALL 4.25 / 5

Coffee rating

The coffee rating is much more than just about the taste of the coffee. It takes into account important 'coffee credentials', including the coffee supplier, equipment used, barista skills and passion, visual appeal of the coffee and many other factors that demonstrate the venue's commitment to coffee excellence.

The following question is the guiding principle used to determine the coffee ratings: **To what extent does this coffee venue deliver an amazing coffee experience?**

Overall rating

In combination with the coffee experience, the overall rating considers to what extent a coffee shop experience delivers a "wow factor" to the customer. Elements that are taken into account include: café environment, ambience, design, scale, customer service and food quality.

To determine a coffee shop's overall rating, the following question is used as the guiding principle: **How does the combination of coffee and the coffee shop experience translate into exceptional levels of customer excitement?**

The London Coffee Guide includes coffee carts and kiosks, as well as coffee shops. It was not considered fair to compare these venues with permanent cafés, so these venues have not been scored. The ten best carts and kiosks in London have been grouped into a separate chapter (p71).

Venues marked as 'NEW' are new to this edition of the guide.

Symbols used throughout The London Coffee Guide

Roaster

Alternative brew methods available

Coffee beans sold on site

Gluten-free products available

Venue has a loyalty card

Soya milk available

Toilets

Parent & baby friendly

Disabled access

Wifi available

Licensed

Coffee courses available

Outdoor seating

A Brief History of London Coffee Shops

THE EARLY YEARS

800 AD The coffee plant (Coffea) attracts human interest and consumption as early as 800 AD in the Kaffe region of Ethiopia. According to legend, it was an Ethiopian goat herder named Kaldi who first discovered how animated his herd of goats became after chewing on the red berries.

MID 17TH CENTURY

Travellers to Middle Eastern areas such as the Ottoman Empire bring coffee to Europe and Britain.

1650 The first English coffee house is established in Oxford by a Jewish gentleman named Jacob at the Angel in the parish of St Peter.

Coffee houses become meeting places for political and literary debates between artists, intellectuals, merchants and bankers. Such venues are known as Penny Universities, in reference to the one penny entrance fee. They are closely associated with reading and provide pamphlets and newspapers, as well as copious amounts of coffee.

1652 London's first coffee house is established by Pasqua Rosée in St Michael's Alley, Cornhill, London EC3.

1668 Edward Lloyd's Coffee House in Lombard Street becomes a key meeting place for ship owners and marine insurance brokers. Situated on the site occupied by Lloyds bank today, this coffee house likely contributed to London becoming a global hub for insurance and financial services.

1674 The Women's Petition Against Coffee is set up in London in response to men spending less time at home due to the "excessive use of the drying and enfeebling liquor".

1675 There are now more than 3,000 coffee houses across England. King Charles II attempts to outlaw coffee houses as hotbeds of revolution, but following large public protests, his proclamation is revoked after 11 days.

1680 Jonathan's Coffee House is established by Jonathan Miles in Change Alley. It is a place where stockbrokers frequently meet and eventually becomes today's London Stock Exchange.

1706 Thomas Twining opens the first known tea room in London, which can still be found at 216 Strand.

18TH CENTURY

Coffee houses gradually decline in popularity and become more elite establishments, when they start charging more than one penny for entrance. Travelling taverns replace coffee houses as popular social spaces. Coffee also becomes a less important commodity as the East India Company and British trade in general focuses more on tea imports from India.

LAST CENTURY

1894 Lyons opens a chain of tea rooms followed by Lyons Corner Houses in London's West End in 1906.

1923 The Kenya Coffee Company Limited (Kenco) is established and soon begins selling coffee on Vere Street, Mayfair.

1950s Italian-run espresso houses featuring Formica-topped tables are a popular feature of this era, particularly in London's Soho.

1952 Moka Bar opens on Frith Street and is London's first espresso bar.

1971 Starbucks opens its first store at Pike Place Market in Seattle, USA.

First Costa Coffee shop opened by brothers Sergio and Bruno Costa at 9 Newport Street, London.

1978 An early pioneer of artisanal coffee, Monmouth Coffee Company opens in Monmouth Street, Covent Garden.

1986 Pret A Manger is established by college friends Julian Metcalf and Sinclair Beecham.

1992 Fairtrade Foundation is established in London by the Catholic Overseas Development Agency, Christian Aid, Oxfam, Traidcraft, the World Development Movement, and the National Federation of Women's Institutes.

1995 Whitbread Group acquires Costa Coffee with 41 stores and a roastery in Lambeth.

1997 Nescafé opens first Café Nescafé trial stores in London and UK, but closes all outlets several years later.

Gerry Ford acquires five Caffè Nero stores and begins building a chain, which grows to become the third-largest coffee shop brand in the UK.

1998 Starbucks launches in the UK, acquiring 65 Seattle Coffee Company stores for an estimated £52 million.

1999 Allegra Strategies releases the groundbreaking Project Café Report, which predicts a significant boom in coffee shops.

LAST DECADE

2000 Internet cafés grow in popularity during the dotcom era.

Marks & Spencer launches Café Revive concept.

2001 The caffè latte is added to the Consumer Price Index (CPI), the basket of goods the government uses to measure products purchased by a typical British household.

2005 Flat White coffee shop opens in Berwick Street, Soho, setting the stage for further Antipodean influences on coffee in the UK.

2006 The number of branded chain coffee shop outlets exceeds 1,000 in London alone.

2007 James Hoffmann is crowned World Barista Champion and founds Square Mile Coffee Roasters.

2008 The first-ever European Coffee Symposium is held at London's Park Lane Hotel.

2009 A host of new artisanal "third wave" coffee shops open in London.

The UK's Gwilym Davies is crowned World Barista Champion.

2010 Costa, Starbucks and several other mainstream coffee chains launch their versions of the flat white.

The World Barista Championships are held in London at Caffè Culture.

The first edition of The London Coffee Guide is published.

2011 Growth of artisanal coffee shops and micro coffee roasteries in London continues to accelerate with the arrival of Workshop (formerly St. Ali), and Prufrock Coffee.

First-ever London Coffee Festival held at the Old Truman Brewery on Brick Lane.

2012 Roastery/cafés increase in popularity with the opening of Caravan King's Cross, Ozone and TAP Wardour Street.

London Coffee Festival hosts UK Barista Championship finals.

Harris + Hoole opens first London store.

West End

London's West End is synonymous with the city's legendary theatre and music scene, as well as its restaurants, shopping and nightlife. Business people and actors rub shoulders with tourists and urbanites, and the area's café culture is just as diverse.

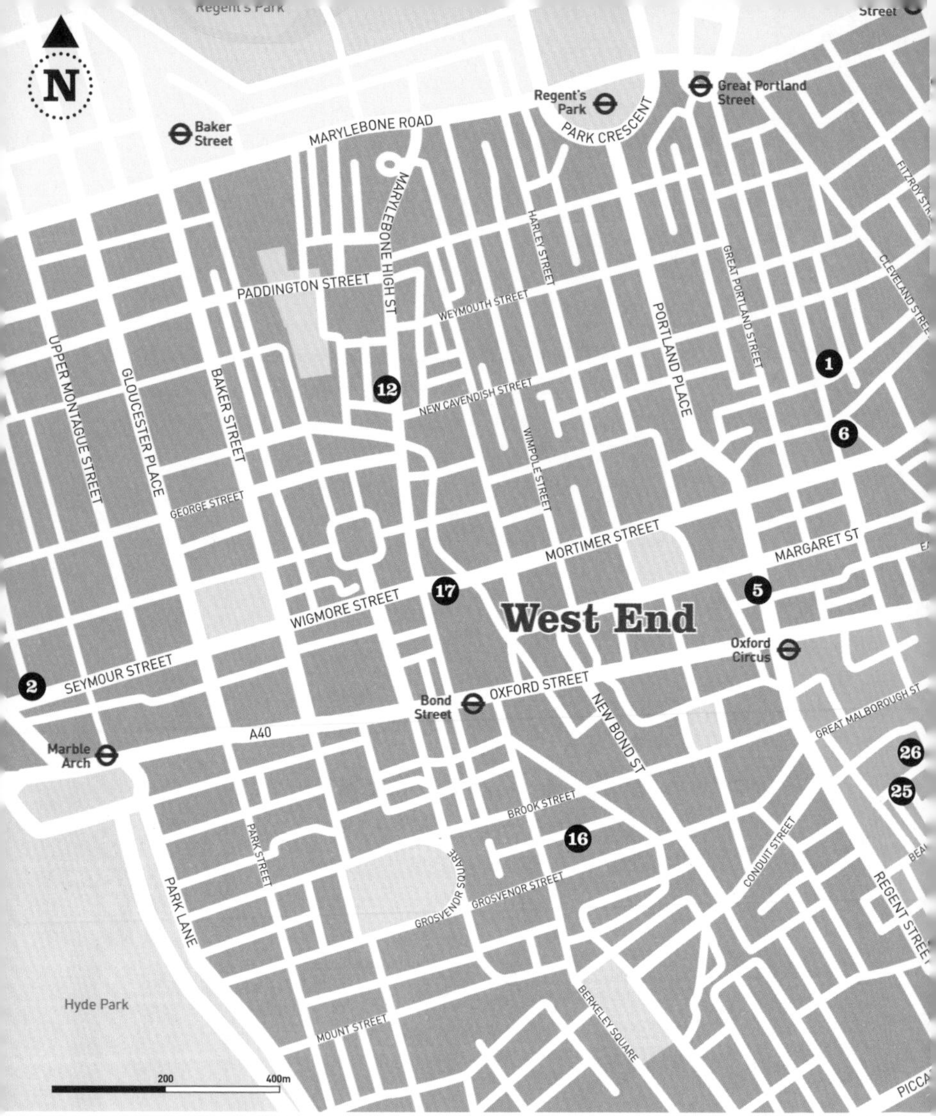

![map of West End coffee venues]

N

Regent's Park

Street

Baker Street

MARYLEBONE ROAD

Regent's Park

Great Portland Street

PARK CRESCENT

PADDINGTON STREET

MARYLEBONE HIGH ST

WEYMOUTH STREET

HARLEY STREET

PORTLAND PLACE

GREAT PORTLAND STREET

CLEVELAND STREET

FITZROY ST

12

NEW CAVENDISH STREET

1

6

GLOUCESTER PLACE

BAKER STREET

GEORGE STREET

WIMPOLE STREET

MORTIMER STREET

MARGARET ST

UPPER MONTAGUE STREET

17

WIGMORE STREET

West End

5

Oxford Circus

2

SEYMOUR STREET

Bond Street

OXFORD STREET

NEW BOND ST

GREAT MARLBOROUGH ST

Marble Arch

A40

26

25

PARK STREET

BROOK STREET

16

CONDUIT STREET

PARK LANE

GROSVENOR SQUARE

GROSVENOR STREET

REGENT STREET

Hyde Park

MOUNT STREET

BERKELEY SQUARE

PICCA

200   400m

Soho

* NEW
◊ TOP 30

The Attendant

27a Foley Street, W1W 6DY

The Attendant is a coffee bar sited in a former Victorian public lavatory. This astonishing conversion has artfully preserved several original features. Suffice to say that the cups and saucers are not the only porcelain the visitor will encounter. Caravan coffee is accompanied by a mouth-watering array of New York deli style sandwiches, which can be ordered through the toilet attendant's old window. Don't be shy to spend a penny or two at one of London's newest and most original coffee venues.

+44(0)20 7637 3794
www.the-attendant.com
⊖ Goodge Street / Oxford Circus

MON-FRI. 7:30am - 5:30pm
SAT-SUN. Closed

First opened 2013
Roaster Caravan
Machine La Marzocco GB/5, 2 groups
Grinder Mazzer Robur E

Espresso £2.40
Cappuccino £2.70
Latte £2.70
Flat white £2.70

MAP REF.

 COFFEE 4.50 / 5  **OVERALL** 4.25 / 5

The Borough Barista

60 Seymour Street, W1H 7JN

Borough Barista provides an artisanal alternative to the high street chains that predominate in West London. This venue on Seymour Street provides a calm oasis of blonde wood and friendly service just around the corner from Marble Arch. The 'St James' espresso blend is custom roasted for Borough Barista, and enjoyed in crisp surroundings by a smart Mayfair crowd. Owner Tim Bloxsome is scheduled to open an eagerly anticipated second venue near Piccadilly in spring 2013.

+44(0)20 7563 7222
www.theboroughbarista.com
⊖ Marble Arch

MON–FRI. 7:30am – 5:00pm
SAT–SUN. 10:00am – 5:00pm

First opened 2011
Roaster Union Hand-Roasted bespoke blend
Machine La Marzocco Linea, 3 groups
Grinder Mazzer Super Jolly, San Remo, Eureka

Espresso £1.70 / £1.90
Cappuccino £2.40 / £2.80
Latte £2.40 / £2.80
Flat white £2.40 / £2.80

MAP REF. **2**

COFFEE 4.25 / 5		OVERALL 4.25 / 5	

Damson Café

64 St. Giles High Street, WC2H 8LE

Unlike its namesake, a tart plum suitable only for jams, Damson Café is a sweet discovery on St Giles High Street. Damson has a comforting country kitchen feel, with reclaimed wooden panelling and stained glass on one wall, a large communal table and white ceramic basins for iced drinks on the counter. Food is made on site, with cakes a particular highlight - try the Victoria sponge with homemade jam. In summer the large windows are opened wide and seating provided on the sunny pavement outside.

+44(0)20 3609 0901
www.damsoncafe.com
⊖ Tottenham Court Road

MON–FRI. 8:00am – 5:30pm
SAT–SUN. 10:00am – 5:30pm

First opened 2012
Roaster Square Mile Coffee Roasters
Machine La Marzocco GB/5, 2 groups
Grinder Mazzer Robur E, Baratza

Espresso £2.20
Cappuccino £2.60
Latte £2.60
Flat white £2.60

MAP REF. **3**

COFFEE 4.25 / 5		OVERALL 4.25 / 5	

Fernandez & Wells Somerset House

Somerset House, Strand, WC2R 1LA

This prestigious venue occupies three rooms in one of London's most beautiful buildings. Customers are treated to the very best of everything: Sicilian panettone, Amalfi lemons, the finest meats, cheeses and wines, artisanal Lithuanian hot chocolate...the list goes on. At the beating heart of the operation are two Synesso Cyncras, handled by a skilled team of baristas, who also prepare delicate single-estate filter coffees. This is more than a café - it is a fine food and coffee emporium.

+44(0)20 7420 9408
www.fernandezandwells.com
⊖ Temple

Sister locations Beak Street / St Anne's Court / Lexington Street / South Kensington

MON-FRI. 8:00am - 10:00pm
SAT. 10:00am - 10:00pm
SUN. 10:00am - 8:00pm

First opened 2011
Roaster Has Bean bespoke blend
Machine Synesso Cyncra, 3 groups x2
Grinder Mazzer

Espresso £2.30
Cappuccino £2.60
Latte £2.60
Flat white £2.60

MAP REF. 4

COFFEE 4.50 / 5

OVERALL 4.50 / 5 ★★★★⯪

Joe & the Juice Regent Street

281 Regent Street, W1B 2HE

This flagship venue for well-established Danish company Joe & the Juice is an entertaining destination that combines an extensive coffee menu with a range of delicious fresh juices and healthy lunch options. The charming staff, comfy sofas and large upstairs lounge-style area make this a vibrant West End location that is always alive with the chatter and excitement of the city.

www.joejuice.com
⊖ Oxford Circus

Sister locations Broadwick Street / King's Road / Dean Street

MON-FRI. 7:30am - 8:30pm
SAT. 9:00am - 8:00pm
SUN. 10:00am - 8:00pm

First opened 2009
Roaster Vida e Caffè
Machine Kees Van Der Westen Mistral, 2 groups
Grinder Mazzer Major E

Espresso £1.55
Cappuccino £2.40
Latte £1.90 / £2.10 / £2.30 / £2.60
Flat white £2.30

MAP REF. **5**

Kaffeine

66 Great Titchfield Street, W1W 7QJ

Since opening in 2009, Kaffeine has established itself as one of London's pre-eminent coffee venues. Australian owner Peter Dore-Smith sets the bar high and his team strives to provide the best café experience possible for all, from casual lunch customers to coffee experts. The coffee bar is distinguished by its impeccable attention to detail, from the stylish wooden interior to the food made fresh on site, and the precise latte art on each carefully crafted coffee. Kaffeine has developed a loyal following, and remains a source for inspiration for London's coffee community.

+44(0)20 7580 6755
www.kaffeine.co.uk
⊖ Oxford Circus

MON-FRI. 7:30am - 6:00pm
SAT. 8:30am - 6:00pm
SUN. 9:30am - 5:00pm

First opened 2009
Roaster Square Mile Coffee Roasters
Machine Synesso Cyncra, 3 groups
Grinder Mazzer Robur E, Anfim

Espresso £1.80 / £2.30
Cappuccino £2.70
Latte £2.70
Flat white £2.60

MAP REF. **6**

  COFFEE 4.75 / 5 OVERALL 5.00 / 5 ★ ★ ★ ★ ★

Lantana

13 Charlotte Place, W1T 1SN

Stylish and understated Fitzrovia favourite Lantana has gone from strength to strength since opening in 2008. This café and eatery is always abuzz with chatter and filled with loyal patrons, particularly during the weekend when its legendary brunch menu has customers queuing out the door. The coffee here is of a consistently high quality, both on the main premises and at the second shopfront next door that caters just for takeaway traffic.

+44(0)20 7637 3347
www.lantanacafe.co.uk
Goodge Street / Tottenham Court Road

Sister locations Salvation Jane

MON-FRI. 8:00am - 6:00pm
SAT-SUN. 9:00am - 5:00pm

First opened 2008
Roaster Square Mile Coffee Roasters
Machine La Marzocco Linea, 3 groups
Grinder Mazzer Robur E, Anfim

Espresso £2.00
Cappuccino £2.60
Latte £2.60
Flat white £2.60

MAP REF.

 COFFEE 4.50 / 5  OVERALL 4.50 / 5

Monmouth Coffee Company Covent Gdn

27 Monmouth Street, WC2H 9EU

This is where the Monmouth phenomenon began, back in 1978. The original Monmouth roastery occupied this site until 2007 when it moved to Bermondsey. The interior here is simple, focusing attention entirely on the coffee. Wooden booths encourage strangers to share space and a chat, and mobile phone use is banned. Monmouth Coffee is nothing short of a London institution, and more often than not, queues of people snake out the door onto the pavement, but it's definitely worth the wait.

+44(0)20 7232 3010
www.monmouthcoffee.co.uk
⊖ Covent Garden

Sister locations The Borough / Bermondsey

MON-SAT. 8:00am - 6:30pm
SUN. Closed

First opened 1978
Roaster Monmouth Coffee Company
Machine La Marzocco Linea, 3 groups
Grinder Mazzer Robur

Espresso £1.35
Cappuccino £2.35
Latte £2.35
Flat white £2.35

MAP REF. **8**

 COFFEE 4.50 / 5  OVERALL 4.50 / 5

New Row Coffee

24 New Row, WC2N 4LA

This miniature coffee house is staffed by a crack team of coffee obsessives who discuss latte art in their downtime and prepare the best flat white on a street crammed with other outlets. Daily filter options are available at the bar, along with an enticing lemon drizzle cake, gourmet cookies and a range of pastries and sandwiches. Fresh almond milk is prepared each day, and the pulp is used to make tasty almond biscuits.

+44(0)20 3583 6949
www.newrowcoffee.co.uk
⊖ Leicester Square

Sister locations Free State Coffee

MON-THU. 7:30am - 7:00pm
FRI. 7:30am - 8:00pm
SAT. 9:00am - 8:00pm
SUN. 9:00am - 6:00pm

First opened 2011
Roaster Union Hand-Roasted
Machine La Marzocco Linea, 3 groups
Grinder Mazzer Major, Mazzer Super Jolly

Espresso £1.60
Cappuccino £2.50
Latte £2.50
Flat white £2.40

MAP REF.

 COFFEE 4.50 / 5  **OVERALL** 4.25 / 5 ★★★★⯨

Notes Covent Garden

36 Wellington Street, WC2E 7BD

Just a stone's throw from the Royal Opera House, this venue is the perfect place for lovers of the arts to browse racks of music and films, or enjoy a delicious homemade pastry. Coffee lovers, however, come here for the Square Mile coffee, single-origin espressos and a range of filter coffees brewed using only the highest-quality water. Notes is much more than just a coffee bar. Tasting evenings for coffee and wine are available to join, and the venue holds a fortnightly live jazz evening.

+44(0)20 7240 7899
www.notes-uk.co.uk
⊖ Covent Garden

Sister locations Trafalgar Square / Tile Yard

MON-WED. 8:00am - 10:00pm
THU-FRI. 8:00am - 11:00pm
SAT. 9:00am - 11:00pm
SUN. 10:00am - 6:00pm

First opened 2011
Roaster Square Mile Coffee Roasters
Machine La Marzocco Strada, 3 groups
Grinder Mazzer Robur E, Anfim

Espresso £2.20 / £2.60
Cappuccino £3.00
Latte £3.00
Flat white £3.00

MAP REF. **10**

COFFEE 4.50 / 5   **OVERALL** 4.25 / 5

Notes Trafalgar Square

31 St Martin's Lane, WC2N 4ER

NEW

Notes Trafalgar Square was the first of three venues opened by Brazilian coffee entrepreneur Fabio Ferreira. Occupying a stunning room with high ceilings, large mirrors and a refined yet welcoming atmosphere, this is a coffee house that looks to London's past for its decor but is distinctly forward-looking in its coffee philosophy. A progressive coffee menu is complemented by a range of fine foods. In the evening, the café converts into a wine bar, and theatre-goers flock here to enjoy the range of excellent wines, spirits, cheeses and charcuterie.

+44(0)20 7240 0424
www.notes-uk.co.uk
⊖ Charing Cross / Leicester Square

Sister locations Tile Yard / Covent Garden

MON-WED. 7:30am - 9:00pm
THU-FRI. 7:00am - 10:00pm
SAT. 9:00am - 10:00pm
SUN. 10:00am - 6:00pm

First opened 2010
Roaster Square Mile Coffee Roasters & others
Machine La Marzocco Strada, 3 groups
Grinder Mazzer Robur, Anfim, Mahlkönig Tanzania

Espresso £1.80 / £2.20
Cappuccino £2.60
Latte £2.60
Flat white £2.60

MAP REF.

 COFFEE 4.50 / 5  **OVERALL** 4.50 / 5

The Providores and Tapa Room

109 Marylebone High Street, W1U 4RX

Run by New Zealand chef Peter Gordon, The Providores is a fusion eatery on upmarket Marylebone High St with a distinctly South Pacific flavour. The venue's ground floor Tapa Room features a huge Rarotongan tapa cloth on one wall and heaves with people from breakfast to dinner, while the dining room upstairs caters for a more formal lunch and dinner crowd. Coffee is supplied by up-and-coming roastery Volcano Coffee Works, and is the perfect accompaniment to a delicious brunch at this popular venue.

+44(0)20 7935 6175
www.theprovidores.co.uk
⊖ Baker Street / Bond Street

Sister locations Kopapa (Covent Garden)

MON-FRI. 9:00am - 11:00pm
SAT. 10:00am - 11:00pm
SUN. 10:00am - 10:30pm

First opened 2001
Roaster Volcano Coffee Works
Machine La Marzocco GB/5, 2 groups
Grinder Mazzer Super Jolly

Espresso £2.00 / £2.40
Cappuccino £2.80
Latte £2.80
Flat white £2.80

MAP REF. **12**

 COFFEE 4.25 / 5   **OVERALL** 4.25 / 5 ★★★★☆

Store Street Espresso

40 Store Street, WC1E 7DB

West End

This exciting venue joined the burgeoning foodie scene on Store Street in 2010 and crowds of hungry students and creatives have been flocking here ever since for the great coffee and electric atmosphere. The café itself is stylish and light-filled, with an ambience that encourages customers to linger for leisure, study or work. A passionate team of baristas serves Square Mile coffee on a new Synesso Hydra, accompanied by a rock soundtrack that perfectly complements the buzz of the venue.

+44(0)20 7637 2623
www.storestreetespresso.com
⊖ Goodge Street

MON–FRI. 7:30am – 7:00pm
SAT. 9:00am – 6:00pm
SUN. 10:00am – 5:00pm

First opened 2010
Roaster Square Mile Coffee Roasters
Machine Synesso Hydra, 2 groups
Grinder Mazzer Robur E, Anfim

Espresso £1.70 / £1.90
Cappuccino £2.40
Latte £2.40
Flat white £2.40

MAP REF.

COFFEE
4.50 / 5

OVERALL
4.50 / 5
★★★★⯪

15

TAP Coffee Rathbone Place

26 Rathbone Place, W1T 1JD

London coffee haven TAP Coffee (formerly named Tapped & Packed) was one of the first coffee bars to offer a selection of espresso blends, as well as an ever-changing menu of filter coffee from artisanal roasters. The Rathbone place store is a popular hangout for Fitzrovia admen, who sip the potent brew whilst masterminding their next advertising campaign. Now roasting beans themselves in nearby Wardour Street, TAP is a fantastic place to witness the artistry of coffee making.

+44(0)20 7580 2163
www.tapcoffee.co.uk
⊖ Tottenham Court Road / Goodge Street

Sister locations Tottenham Court Road / Wardour Street

MON-FRI. 8:00am - 7:00pm
SAT. 10:00am - 6:00pm
SUN. Closed

First opened 2010
Roaster TAP Coffee
Machine Nuova Simonelli Aurelia II T3
Grinder Mazzer Robur E, Mazzer Kony E, Mazzer Super Jolly E

Espresso £2.00
Cappuccino £2.50
Latte £2.50
Flat white £2.50

MAP REF.

COFFEE 4.75 / 5		OVERALL 4.50 / 5	

TAP Coffee Tottenham Court Road

114 Tottenham Court Road, W1T 5AH

TAP Tottenham Court Road boasts a unique Nuova Simonelli Aurelia machine customised with polished wood panels. A glass window on the back panel reveals the intricate workings within. Separate blends are used for espresso and milk coffees, and single origin filters are available from the brew bar. The interior features a tree-stump podium in the centre, washed steel, exposed light bulbs and white ceramic that recall London's Victorian heyday while offering a welcoming space to enjoy cake or a leisurely lunch.

+44(0)20 7580 2163
www.tapcoffee.co.uk
⊖ Warren Street

Sister locations Rathbone Place / Wardour Street

MON–FRI. 8:00am - 7:00pm
SAT. 10:00am - 6:00pm
SUN. Closed

First opened 2011
Roaster TAP Coffee
Machine Customised Nuova Simonelli Aurelia
Grinder Mazzer Robur E, Mazzer Kony E, Mazzer Super Jolly E

Espresso £2.00
Cappuccino £2.50
Latte £2.50
Flat white £2.50

MAP REF.

 COFFEE 4.50 / 5

 OVERALL 4.50 / 5 ★★★★⯪

Taylor Street Baristas Mayfair

22 Brooks Mews, W1K 4DY

Hidden away down a little mews, Taylor St Mayfair is popular with be-suited professionals. Regulars vie for top position on the 'Super frequent coffee freaks' blackboard behind the counter. It's not just the hedge fund managers who have a healthy competitive streak; head barista Magda Grzelka is a UK Barista Championship competitor. With such a talented team, it's no surprise that the coffee continues to impress. Taylor St remains very much at the forefront of the London coffee scene.

+44(0)20 7629 3163
www.taylor-st.com
⊖ Bond Street

Sister locations Richmond / Liverpool Street / Shoreditch / Canary Wharf / Monument / Bank / South Quay

MON-FRI. 8:00am - 5:00pm
SAT. Closed
SUN. Closed

First opened 2011
Roaster Union Hand-Roasted and others
Machine La Marzocco Linea, 3 groups
Grinder Mazzer Kony E, Mazzer Super Jolly, Anfim

Espresso £2.00
Cappuccino £3.00
Latte £3.00
Flat white £3.00

MAP REF. 16

 COFFEE 4.50 / 5  **OVERALL** 4.50 / 5

Workshop Coffee Co. Marylebone

75 Wigmore Street, W1U 1QD

West End

At this smaller outpost of Workshop Coffee Co. (formerly named Sensory Lab), coffee is a science and its baristas are laureates of the highest order. This is coffee at its best, brewed with clinical precision and minute attention to detail. This location provides the blueprint for a new kind of coffee bar, with a sleek marble and dark wood interior, simple bar-style seating, a small range of pastries enshrined behind polished glass and a range of Workshop beans and coffee-making equipment available to buy.

+44(0)20 7253 5754
www.workshopcoffee.com
⊖ Bond Street

Sister locations Clerkenwell

MON-FRI. 7:00am - 7:00pm
SAT-SUN. 9:00am - 6:00pm

First opened 2011
Roaster Workshop Coffee Co.
Machine Synesso Hydra, 3 groups
Grinder Mazzer Robur x2, Mazzer Major, Mahlkönig Tanzania

Espresso £2.00
Cappuccino £2.80
Latte £3.00
Flat white £2.50

MAP REF.

 COFFEE 4.75 / 5  **OVERALL** 4.50 / 5

How can something so *indulgently* *creamy* be so *low in saturated fat?*

That's the beauty of an Alproccino. All the taste and texture of a cappuccino without the merest hint of animal fat. Deliciously low in saturated fat yet positively brimming with pure plant goodness.

feed your curiosity *enjoy plant power*

Soho

Famous for its outrageous nightlife, Soho is also well-known for its cutting-edge bars, clubs and restaurants. This spirit of experimentation and adventure extends to coffee and many of London's most exciting artisanal cafés can be found here.

Fernandez & Wells Beak Street

73 Beak Street, W1F 9SR

This venue perfects Fernandez & Wells' signature combination of artisanal European food with superb coffee. Fernandez & Wells was one of the first coffee bars in London to install the high-end Synesso Cyncra espresso machine. Now with several sister shops, this café retains its simple focus on fine coffee and food. The clean interior accentuates this priority with unadorned cream walls and rustic timber benches. Fernandez & Wells retains its position as a premier London coffee and foodie destination.

+44(0)20 7287 8124
www.fernandezandwells.com
⊖ Piccadilly Circus / Oxford Circus

Sister locations St Anne's Court / Lexington Street / South Kensington / Somerset House

MON-FRI. 7:30am - 6:00pm
SAT. 9:00am - 6:00pm
SUN. 10:00am - 5:00pm

First opened 2007
Roaster Has Bean bespoke blend
Machine Synesso Cyncra, 3 groups
Grinder Mazzer Robur, Mazzer Robur E, Ditting

Espresso £2.30
Cappuccino £2.60
Latte £2.60
Flat white £2.60

MAP REF. 18

 COFFEE 4.75 / 5  **OVERALL** 4.50 / 5

Flat White

17 Berwick Street, W1F 0PT

Flat White has been firmly established as a London institution since opening in 2005 with the aim of introducing Antipodean-style coffee to London. A mecca for Kiwis and Aussies longing for a taste of home, Flat White also introduced many native Londoners to the antipodean drink from which the café takes its name. The venue may also be the only venue in town to serve a custom-roasted Square Mile blend, expertly pulled through a 4-group Synesso Hydra (affectionately dubbed "The Orca").

+44(0)20 7734 0370
www.flatwhitecafe.com
⊖ Oxford Circus / Tottenham Court Road

MON-FRI. 8:00am - 7:00pm
SAT-SUN. 9:00am - 6:00pm

First opened 2005
Roaster Square Mile Coffee Roasters bespoke blend
Machine Synesso Hydra, 4 groups
Grinder Mazzer Robur E, Mazzer Robur, Anfim

Espresso £2.00
Cappuccino £2.50
Latte £2.50
Flat white £2.50

MAP REF.

COFFEE 4.75 / 5

OVERALL 4.50 / 5 ★★★★✫

Foxcroft & Ginger

3 Berwick Street, W1F 0DR

This stylish Soho coffee house is now a key feature of the vibrant Berwick St community. A heavy wooden door leads into an industrial space decorated with a mixture of concrete, tile, brick and exposed piping, and the downstairs area offers a welcome retreat. Caravan espresso is made using a shiny Synesso Cyncra and perfectly complements the range of locally sourced food on offer, which includes gourmet sandwiches.

+44(0)20 3602 3371
www.foxcroftandginger.co.uk
⊖ Piccadilly Circus

MON. 8:00am - 7:00pm
TUE-FRI. 8:00am - 10:00pm
SAT. 9:00am - 10:00pm
SUN. 9:00am - 7:00pm

First opened 2010
Roaster Caravan, Has Bean
Machine Synesso Cyncra, 3 groups
Grinder Anfim x2

Espresso £2.00
Cappuccino £2.50
Latte £2.50
Flat white £2.50

MAP REF. 20

 COFFEE 4.50 / 5  OVERALL 4.25 / 5

Ginger & White Soho

1 Silver Place, W1F 0JW

NEW

Soho brims with superb coffee bars, so newcomers must show exceptional flair to compete for the area's quality-conscious customers. Ginger & White meets this challenge with aplomb, marrying beautiful Square Mile coffee with a marvellous selection of artisan food and baked goodies. Patriotic provisions include cheddar and Marmite toasties, and gloriously sticky Chelsea buns. The Soho inspired interior lends it a more creative edge than its sister shops, but retains the fabulously British panache for which Ginger & White is best loved.

+44(0)20 7734 5374
www.gingerandwhite.com
⊖ Piccadilly Circus / Oxford Circus

Sister locations Belsize Park / Hampstead

MON-FRI. 8:30am - 6:00pm
SAT. 10:30am - 6:30pm
SUN. Closed

First opened 2012
Roaster Square Mile Coffee Roasters, Climpson & Sons
Machine La Marzocco FB/80, 3 groups
Grinder Mazzer Robur E x2, Mazzer Super Jolly

Espresso £2.00
Cappuccino £2.70
Latte £2.70
Flat white £2.70

MAP REF. 21

 COFFEE 4.50 / 5  OVERALL 4.50 / 5 ★★★★✦

Nude Espresso Soho

19 Soho Square, W1D 3QN

Nude Espresso's signature East blend coffee has arrived in Soho. The interior here is sleeker and more understated than Nude Hanbury Street, but the staff are just as passionate about delivering excellent coffee to their urbane Soho customers. A range of tasty breakfast, lunch and sweet foods are prepared fresh by Nude chefs in the open kitchen. A selection of coffee equipment is also available to purchase, and Nude runs home brewing workshops to help customers get the most from their gear.

+44(0)7712 899 336
www.nudeespresso.com
⊖ Tottenham Court Road

Sister locations Hanbury Street / Nude Roastery (Old Truman Brewery)

MON-FRI. 8:00am - 5:00pm
SAT-SUN. 10:00am - 6:00pm

First opened 2011
Roaster Nude Coffee Roasters
Machine La Marzocco Linea, 2 groups
Grinder Compak K-10

Espresso £2.00
Cappuccino £2.50
Latte £2.50
Flat white £2.50

MAP REF. **22**

COFFEE 4.50 / 5		OVERALL 4.25 / 5	★★★★☆

Princi

135 Wardour Street, W1F 0UT

A buzzing, lively eatery, Princi is a perfect fit for Soho and is packed with hungry customers all hours of the day and night. One length of the venue is occupied by tantalising displays of croissants, tarts, cakes, pizza and salads all made on site. The elegant dining area consists of granite tables and a long metal bench against a water-feature wall, and the large window frontage is perfect for people-watching on this entertaining street. Coffee is supplied by Brighton's Small Batch Coffee Company.

+44(0)20 7478 8888
www.princi.co.uk
⊖ Oxford Circus / Tottenham Court Road

MON-SAT. 8:00am - 12:00am
SUN. 8:30am - 10:00pm

First opened 2008
Roaster Small Batch Coffee Company
Machine La Marzocco Linea, 3 groups
Grinder Mazzer Robur

Espresso £1.60
Cappuccino £2.30
Latte £2.30
Flat white £2.40

MAP REF. **23**

COFFEE 3.75 / 5	OVERALL 4.25 / 5	★★★★☆

Rapha Cycle Club

85 Brewer Street, W1F 9ZN

The perfectionism Rapha applies to its cycling gear is readily apparent in its approach to coffee. The espresso here is truly extraordinary. Try a shot made with German JB or Swedish Drop Coffee (both a rarity in London), pulled through a customised Synesso Hydra. Bike locks are available for those arriving on two wheels, and the vintage Italian cycling memorabilia makes a fascinating addition. Coffee is no afterthought here; Rapha has established itself as a coffee destination in its own right.

+44(0)20 7494 9831
www.rapha.cc
⊖ Piccadilly Circus

MON-FRI. 7:30am - 9:00pm
SAT. 8:30am - 7:00pm
SUN. 10:00am - 6:00pm

First opened 2012
Roaster JB Kaffee, Drop Coffee Roasters
Machine Synesso Hydra, 2 groups
Grinder Anfim x2, Mahlkönig Tanzania

Espresso £2.00 / £2.50
Flat white £2.75 / £3.00

MAP REF. **24**

 COFFEE 4.50 / 5 OVERALL 4.50 / 5 ★★★★⯪

27

Sacred Ganton Street

13 Ganton Street, W1F 9BL

The Sacred empire now extends across six London locations but this is where it all began back in 2005. Owners Tubbs Wanigasekera and Matt Clark are proud New Zealanders and this shines through in the decor and relaxed atmosphere that characterises this busy café. While the main upstairs area has a pleasing openness that extends out into the bustle of Carnaby Street, couches in the mellow basement area offer a cosy refuge in which to sip a cup of the delicious New Zealand-style house roast.

+44(0)20 7734 1415
www.sacredcafe.com
⊖ Oxford Circus

Sister locations Covent Garden / Highbury Studios / Westfield / Kingly Court / Torrington Place

MON–FRI. 7:30am – 8:00pm
SAT–SUN. 10:00am – 7:00pm

First opened 2005
Roaster Sacred House Roast
Machine La Marzocco Linea, 3 groups
Grinder Anfim Super Caimano, Mazzer Super Jolly

Espresso £1.60
Cappuccino £2.60 / £2.80
Latte £2.60 / £2.80
Flat white £2.60 / £2.80

MAP REF. **25**

 COFFEE 4.50 / 5      **OVERALL** 4.50 / 5

Speakeasy Espresso & Brew Bar

3 Lowndes Court, W1F 7HD

Occupying a light, modern space just off Carnaby Street, Speakeasy is home to some of London's most talented baristas. There's more to this stylish coffee bar than meets the eye. Speakeasy encourages a hands-on approach to coffee making, operating a coffee school in their dedicated brew bar downstairs. In addition, free drop-in sessions are run on Thursdays 5-7pm, where budding home baristas can seek advice and get hands-on with a range of equipment from cold water drippers to a domestic Rocket espresso machine.

www.speakeasycoffee.co.uk
 Oxford Circus

Sister locations Department of Coffee and Social Affairs / The Liberty of Norton Folgate / Chancery Coffee

MON-FRI. 7:30am - 7:00pm
SAT. 10:00am - 8:00pm
SUN. 10:00am - 6:00pm

First opened 2011
Roaster Climpson & Sons and others
Machine La Marzocco FB/80, 3 groups
Grinder Mazzer Robur E x2, Mazzer Super Jolly, Mahlkönig Tanzania

Espresso £2.00
Cappuccino £2.60 / £2.90
Latte £2.60 / £2.90
Flat white £2.40

MAP REF.

TAP Coffee Wardour Street

193 Wardour Street, W1F 8ZF

Formerly known as Tapped & Packed, TAP Coffee's newest venue is an impressive statement in coffee bar design. Two rows of perfectly aligned tables draw the eye towards the magnificent Probat roaster. Low-hung spotlights highlight the interior's bare wood and gleaming gunmetal fixtures. TAP now serves its excellent house-roasted 'Queen of Clubs' blend and single origins at the dedicated brew bar. Connoisseurs will also appreciate the green tea offered as a palate cleanser. Visitors can expect exceptionally high standards from one of London's newest but most accomplished coffee destinations.

+44(0)20 7580 2163
www.tapcoffee.co.uk
⊖ Tottenham Court Road

Sister locations Rathbone Place / Tottenham Court Road

MON-FRI. 8:00am - 7:00pm
SAT. 10:00am - 6:00pm
SUN. 12:00am - 6:00pm

First opened 2012
Roaster TAP Coffee
Machine Nuova Simonelli Aurelia II T3, 3 groups
Grinder Mazzer Robur E, Mazzer Kony E, Mazzer Super Jolly E

Espresso £2.00
Cappuccino £2.50
Latte £2.50
Flat white £2.50

MAP REF.

 COFFEE 4.75 / 5    **OVERALL** 4.75 / 5

LA MARZOCCO

FINELY CRAFTED

— MADE IN ITALY —

" WHY LA MARZOCCO?
FOR OUR UNIQUE PHILOSOPHY,
DISTINCT HERITAGE,
ULTIMATE TECHNOLOGY
AND ITALIAN DESIGN."

Farringdon & Clerkenwell

Formerly hubs of manufacturing and enterprise, the districts of Farringdon and Clerkenwell now house smart offices, loft apartments, night clubs and restaurants. Some of the most exciting coffee venues in town can also be found here, making this the new heart of London's burgeoning coffee culture.

Caravan Exmouth Market

11-13 Exmouth Market, EC1R 4QD

Caravan roastery and restaurant is a popular fixture on the diverse Exmouth Market food and coffee scene. This modern dining venue is always busy, particularly on sunny days when patrons spill out onto the pavement. Plenty of options on the menu make this a popular destination for a weekend brunch or casual dinner. As well as espresso, a wide variety of coffee brewing methods are on offer, allowing patrons to appreciate the full range of flavours found in Caravan house roasts.

+44(0)20 7833 8115
www.caravanonexmouth.co.uk
⊖ Angel / Farringdon

Sister locations King's Cross

MON-WED. 8:00am - 11:00pm
THU-FRI. 8:00am - 12:00am
SAT. 10:00am - 12:00am
SUN. 10:00am - 10:30pm

First opened 2010
Roaster Caravan
Machine La Marzocco Linea, 3 groups
Grinder Mazzer Robur E x2, Mazzer Super Jolly, Ditting KR1403

Espresso £1.60
Cappuccino £2.40
Latte £2.40
Flat white £2.40

MAP REF.

Department of Coffee and Social Affairs

14-16 Leather Lane, EC1N 7SU

Part of the The Coffeesmiths Collective, Department of Coffee and Social Affairs is a key player on the booming Farringdon coffee scene. Occupying a former ironmonger's premises across two shopfronts on Leather Lane, this generous space features an unpolished wood and exposed brick theme with plentiful seating. The Department offers an alternative to the Square Mile coffee served by most in the vicinity. The Climpson & Sons espresso is supplemented by alternating guest blends.

www.departmentofcoffee.co.uk
Farringdon / Chancery Lane

Sister locations Speakeasy Espresso & Brew Bar / The Liberty of Norton Folgate / Chancery Coffee

MON-FRI. 7:00am - 6:00pm
SAT-SUN. 10:00am - 4:00pm

First opened 2010
Roaster Climpson & Sons bespoke blend and others
Machine La Marzocco FB/80, 3 groups
Grinder Mazzer Robur E x2, Mazzer Super Jolly

Espresso £2.00
Cappuccino £2.50 / £2.80
Latte £2.50 / £2.80
Flat white £2.30

MAP REF.

COFFEE 4.50 / 5	OVERALL 4.25 / 5
	★★★★

Farm Collective Farringdon

91 Cowcross Street, EC1M 6BH

Farm Collective takes pride in sourcing high-quality, fresh, ethical produce directly from British farms. This emphasis on quality extends to the coffee - excellent Square Mile espresso is pulled through a Synesso Cyncra and can be enjoyed along with a signature peanut butter brownie. Farm also offers Tregothnan teas, the only tea grown in England. The tantalising food display makes this a great destination for a quick drop-in or a hearty lunch menu is available if a lazy lunch is more your speed.

+44(0)20 7253 2142
www.farmcollective.com
⊖ Farringdon

Sister locations Bank

MON-FRI. 7:00am - 3:30pm
SAT-SUN. Closed

First opened 2009
Roaster Square Mile Coffee Roasters
Machine Synesso Cyncra, 2 groups
Grinder Anfim

Espresso £1.70 / £2.10
Cappuccino £2.10 / £2.40
Latte £2.10 / £2.40
Flat white £2.20 / £2.50

MAP REF. **30**

COFFEE
4.25 / 5

OVERALL
4.00 / 5
★★★★☆

Ground Control

61 Amwell Street, EC1R 1UR

The Ethiopian Coffee Company's mission is to showcase the very best coffees from this unique part of Africa, including Yirgacheffe, Harrar and Sidamo. The company's Clerkenwell café, Ground Control, combines traditional Ethiopian curios with the sharp, space-age lines of a Kees Van Der Westen Mirage coffee machine. The Ethiopian Coffee Company also sells its beans at the Real Food Market behind the Southbank Centre (Fridays-Sundays) and Partridges Specialist Food Market in Chelsea (Saturdays).

+44(0)20 7502 1201
www.theethiopiancoffeecompany.co.uk
⊖ Angel

MON-SAT. 8:00am - 4:00pm
SUN. 9:00am - 4:00pm

First opened 2012
Roaster The Ethiopian Coffee Company
Machine Kees Van Der Westen Mirage, 2 groups
Grinder Mazzer Super Jolly

Espresso £2.25
Cappuccino £2.50
Latte £2.50
Flat white £2.50

MAP REF. **31**

Prufrock Coffee

23-25 Leather Lane, EC1N 7TE

Photo: Micha Theiner

Prufrock Coffee has achieved cult status in London, and international recognition for its progressive methods and tireless pursuit of coffee excellence. Founded by Gwilym Davies (2009 World Barista Champion) and Jeremy Challender, Prufrock is a premier destination to see unusual brew methods and sample rare coffees. The space also incorporates the Barista Resource And Training school (BRAT). The extremely knowledgeable staff are welcoming and enthusiastic about their craft. Prufrock's pop-up bar at Present has now popped down, and the magnificent Victoria Arduino lever machine has moved to Leather Lane.

+44(0)20 7242 0467
www.prufrockcoffee.com
Farringdon / Chancery Lane

MON-FRI. 8:00am - 6:00pm
SAT. 10:00am - 5:00pm
SUN. 10:00am - 5:00pm

First opened 2011
Roaster Square Mile Coffee Roasters and others
Machine Nuova Simonelli Aurelia II T3, Victoria Arduino Athena Leva
Grinder Mahlkönig Tanzania, Mahlkönig K30, Nuova Simonelli Mythos

Espresso £2.20 / £2.60
Cappuccino £2.80 / £3.20
Latte £3.00 / £3.40
Flat white £2.80 / £3.20

MAP REF.

 COFFEE 5.00 / 5    **OVERALL** 4.75 / 5

38

Workshop Coffee Co. Clerkenwell

27 Clerkenwell Road, EC1M 5RN

Formerly known as St Ali, Workshop Coffee has experienced a meteoric rise. This temple to speciality coffee contains a café, restaurant and roastery, spanning multiple floors of an industrial themed space. A remarkable 'living wall' of plants adds a dash of green to the raw brick and steel. Attracting top talent from the UK, Australia and the US, Workshop is a young company with a reputation for roasting excellence. An array of single origins and the popular 'Cult of Done' espresso blend are crafted on-site, and their coffee is now a frequent sight in some of the capital's finest coffee bars.

+44(0)20 7253 5754
www.workshopcoffee.com
⊖ Farringdon

Sister locations Marylebone

MON. 7:30am – 6:00pm
TUE-FRI. 7:30am – 10:00pm
SAT-SUN. 8:00am – 6:00pm

First opened 2011
Roaster Workshop Coffee Co.
Machine Synesso Cyncra, 3 groups,
La Marzocco Linea, 2 groups
Grinder Mazzer Robur E x2, Mazzer Major E,
Mahlkönig Tanzania

Espresso £2.20
Cappuccino £2.80
Latte £3.00
Flat white £3.00

MAP REF. 33

COFFEE 5.00 / 5 🫘🫘🫘🫘🫘 **OVERALL 4.75 / 5** ★★★★✯

The City

London's centre of finance and commerce may not boast the sheer number of cafés as Soho or the West End, but several recent high-profile openings have rapidly transformed its coffee fortunes. The City is surprisingly quiet at weekends (and many coffee bars open Monday to Friday only), so the area is best experienced during the bustling work week.

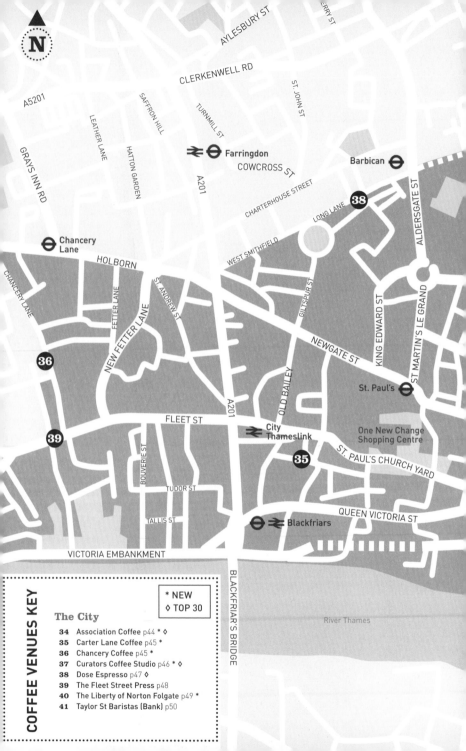

AYLESBURY ST

CLERKENWELL RD

A5201

SAFFRON HILL

TURNMILL ST

ST. JOHN ST

LEATHER LANE

HATTON GARDEN

⇒ ⊖ **Farringdon**

COWCROSS ST

Barbican ⊖

GRAYS INN RD

A201

CHARTERHOUSE STREET

38

ALDERSGATE ST

⊖ **Chancery Lane**

HOLBORN

WEST SMITHFIELD

LONG LANE

CHANCERY LANE

FETTER LANE

ST ANDREW ST

NEW FETTER LANE

GILTSPUR ST

NEWGATE ST

KING EDWARD ST

ST MARTIN'S LE GRAND

36

OLD BAILEY

St. Paul's ⊖

One New Change Shopping Centre

39

FLEET ST

A201

⇒ **City Thameslink**

35

ST. PAUL'S CHURCH YARD

BOUVERIE ST

TUDOR ST

TALLIS ST

⊖ ⇒ **Blackfriars**

QUEEN VICTORIA ST

VICTORIA EMBANKMENT

BLACKFRIAR'S BRIDGE

River Thames

Association Coffee

10–12 Creechurch Lane, EC3A 5AY

Association brings gourmet coffee and quality food from small suppliers to the heart of the City. A meticulously prepared range of pastries, cakes and sandwiches are served in sleek, yet accessible surroundings. The interior follows a familiar industrial template, but adds City-influenced twists including a tiled communal table studded with banker's lamps, offering a great spot for meetings or casual lunches. Association's brew bar is a particular feature, manned by professional baristas who are serious about their craft.

+44(0)20 7283 1155
www.londoncoffeeproject.com
⊖ Aldgate / Liverpool Street

MON-FRI. 7:30am – 5:30pm
SAT-SUN. Closed

First opened 2012
Roaster Square Mile Coffee Roasters, Has Bean, Workshop Coffee Co.
Machine Synesso Hydra, 3 groups
Grinder Mazzer Robur E, Mazzer Kony E, Mahlkönig Tanzania

Espresso £2.10
Cappuccino £2.60
Latte £2.60
Flat white £2.60

MAP REF. 34

 COFFEE 4.75 / 5  **OVERALL** 4.50 / 5

Carter Lane Coffee

50 Carter Lane, EC4V 5EA

Nestled in one of London's narrowest streets, this pint-sized coffee bar means business. Sitting proudly on the immaculate counter is a high end Synesso Hydra. Climpson & Sons supply the beans, and head barista Anita is a skilled hand (she also presides over the Blooming Good Coffee kiosk at Columbia Road market). A small selection of pastries and cookies are also available. Carter Lane successfully blends East End coffee expertise with a clean-cut style sharper than a city boy's lapels.

+44(0)20 7248 9493
⊖ St Paul's / ⇌ City Thameslink

MON-FRI. 7:30am - 4:00pm
SAT-SUN. Closed

First opened 2012
Roaster Climpson & Sons
Machine Synesso Hydra, 2 groups
Grinder Mazzer Robur, Mazzer Mini

Espresso £1.30 / £1.50
Cappuccino £2.30
Latte £2.30
Flat white £2.30

MAP REF. **35**

 COFFEE 4.50 / 5  **OVERALL 4.25 / 5** ★ ★ ★ ★

Chancery Coffee

90 Chancery Lane, WC2A 1DT

Chancery Coffee's friendly baristas demonstrate meticulous attention to detail at the controls of their bright red La Marzocco FB/80. The magnificent copper counter forms the focal point in the small space. In an honourable nod to the professional associations of barristers, the café's branding incorporates the four emblematic creatures of the Inns of Court. The coffee is made to a consistently excellent standard, but with seating restricted to a narrow bench, we suggest having yours to go.

www.chancerycoffee.co.uk
⊖ Chancery Lane

Sister locations Department of Coffee and Social Affairs / Speakeasy Espresso & Brew Bar / The Liberty of Norton Folgate

MON-FRI. 7:30am - 5:00pm
SAT-SUN. Closed

First opened 2012
Roaster Climpson & Sons bespoke blend
Machine La Marzocco FB/80
Grinder Mazzer Robur E, Mazzer Super Jolly E

Espresso £2.00
Cappuccino £2.60 / £2.80
Latte £2.60 / £2.80
Flat white £2.40

MAP REF. **36**

 COFFEE 4.25 / 5  **OVERALL 4.25 / 5** ★ ★ ★ ★

Curators Coffee Studio

9a Cullum Street, EC3M 7JJ

There's a fine line between coffee and art at this small City café from former Kaffeine barista Catherine Seay. The vibrant turquoise La Marzocco Strada and matching grinders contrast with reclaimed wooden furniture and a vintage filing cabinet. Artworks by staff and customers adorn the walls, and selected take-out cups feature art by Curators barista and illustrator Tim Shaw. The superb coffee is accompanied by irresistible cakes from Bittersweet Bakers and pastries from Yeast Bakery.

+44(0)20 7283 4642
www.curatorscoffee.com
Monument / Bank

MON-FRI. 7:30am - 5:00pm
SAT-SUN. Closed

First opened 2012
Roaster Union Hand-Roasted, Square Mile Coffee Roasters
Machine La Marzocco Strada, 3 groups
Grinder Mazzer Robur E, Mazzer Mini, Anfim

Espresso £2.00
Cappuccino £2.60
Latte £2.60
Flat white £2.60

MAP REF. **37**

COFFEE 4.50 / 5		OVERALL 4.50 / 5	
		OVERALL 4.50 / 5	★★★★⯪

46

Dose Espresso

70 Long Lane, EC1A 9EJ

Straddling the border between the City and Farringdon, Dose Espresso is recognised as a leader in London's artisanal coffee scene. Owner and barista James Phillips sets a high standard in his small but welcoming espresso bar. All Dose coffee, milk and ingredients are ethically sourced and environmental consciousness is an important part of the company's identity. The café features a striking red, black and white colour scheme, which extends to the seductive curves of the Florentine FB/80 machine.

+44(0)20 7600 0382
www.dose-espresso.com
⊖ Barbican

MON–FRI. 7:00am – 5:00pm
SAT. 9:00am – 4:00pm
SUN. Closed

First opened 2009
Roaster Square Mile Coffee Roasters and others
Machine La Marzocco FB/80, 3 groups
Grinder Ceado E92, Anfim Super Caimano, Mahlkönig Vario

Espresso £1.70 / £2.00
Cappuccino £2.50 / £3.00
Latte £2.40 / £2.90
Flat white £2.50 / £3.00

MAP REF. **38**

 **COFFEE** 4.75 / 5

 **OVERALL** 4.25 / 5 ★★★★⯪

The Fleet Street Press

3 Fleet Street, EC4Y 1AU

The Fleet Street Press (formerly Get Coffee) occupies a listed building on Fleet Street, serving a mixed crowd of lawyers, bankers, students and tourists. Head barista Davide Pastorino oversees a friendly team pulling shots on a heavily modified La Spaziale S5, and the Butterworth & Son blend offers a pleasing change of pace. The refreshed interior retains a stunning stained glass window on the staircase leading to a lower level seating area, a perfect refuge from the clatter of the city outside.

+44(0)20 7583 7757
⊖ Temple

MON–FRI. 6:30am – 6:30pm
SAT. 9:30am – 5:00pm
SUN. Closed

First opened 2011
Roaster Butterworth & Son
Machine La Spaziale S5 PID, 2 groups
Grinder Mahlkönig K30 Vario

Espresso £1.80
Cappuccino £2.20 / £2.50
Latte £ 2.20 / £2.50
Flat white £2.40

MAP REF. **39**

 COFFEE 4.00 / 5  **OVERALL** 4.00 / 5

The Liberty of Norton Folgate

201 Bishopgate, Norton Folgate, EC2M 3UG

This café is named after a tiny self-governing area of East London that spanned just a few blocks up until 1855 and still gives its name to a short stretch of the A10. The narrow, sun-filled venue features a takeaway zone at one end and an eat-in area at the other. Custom-made lights inspired by the molecular structure of caffeine combine with minimal black-and-white decor, high ceilings and huge windows to create a serene, crystalline space. Guest coffees and a variety of brewing methods are on offer.

www.libertyofnortonfolgate.co.uk
Liverpool Street / Shoreditch High Street

Sister locations Department of Coffee and Social Affairs / Speakeasy Espresso & Brew Bar / Chancery Coffee

MON-FRI. 7:00am - 5:30pm
SAT-SUN. 10:00am - 4:00pm

First opened 2012
Roaster Climpson & Sons bespoke blend
Machine La Marzocco FB/80, 3 groups
Grinder Mazzer Robur E x2

Espresso £2.00
Cappuccino £2.60
Latte £2.60
Flat white £2.40

MAP REF. **40**

COFFEE
4.25 / 5

OVERALL
4.25 / 5 ★★★★

Taylor St Baristas Bank

125 Old Broad Street, EC2N 1AR

Taylor St Baristas' Bank venue is one of the largest and busiest cafés in its rapidly growing family of venues. The sleek and spacious design includes lofty ceilings, timber finishings and designer drop lights that make this a great place for a business meeting or lunchtime escape. The daily menu is projected onto the wall behind the bar and includes a rotating menu of fresh, antipodean-style food.

+44(0)20 7256 8665
www.taylor-st.com
Bank / Liverpool Street

Sister locations Richmond / Liverpool Street / Shoreditch / Canary Wharf / Monument / Mayfair / South Quay

MON-FRI. 7:00am – 6:00pm
SAT-SUN. Closed

First opened 2010
Roaster Union Hand-Roasted and others
Machine Nuova Simonelli Aurelia T3
Grinder Mazzer Robur E x2, Ditting 1203

Espresso £1.80
Cappuccino £2.50 / £2.90 / £3.80
Latte £2.50 / £2.90 / £3.80
Flat white £2.50 / £3.40

MAP REF. 41

 COFFEE 4.50 / 5  **OVERALL** 4.25 / 5

Handmade
in Milan, Italy.

Camden & Islington

Stretching from the banks of the Thames to the leafy streets of Hampstead, the districts of Camden and Islington contain a huge variety of cafés and restaurants, from the stylish venues of Holborn to the colourful market stalls of Camden and chic North London delis.

Camden & Islington

Bea's of Bloomsbury Theobald's Road

44 Theobald's Road, WC1X 8NW

The selection of baked goods and treats on display at Bea's is enough to make any cake-lover go weak at the knees. Customers can purchase a selection of cakes to go, or enjoy lunch or afternoon tea while watching the bakery's famous treats being created in the kitchen at the rear of the café. Fresh Square Mile coffee provides the perfect accompaniment for a decadent chocolate cupcake or even a slice of espresso bourbon cake for a double caffeine hit.

+44(0)20 7242 8330
www.beasofbloomsbury.com
⊖ Chancery Lane / Holborn

Sister locations One New Change / Maltby Street Market

MON-FRI. 8:00am - 7:00pm
SAT-SUN. 12:00pm - 7:00pm

First opened 2008
Roaster Square Mile Coffee Roasters
Machine La Marzocco Linea, 2 groups
Grinder Anfim, Mazzer

Espresso £1.70 / £2.00
Cappuccino £2.40 / £2.70
Latte £2.40 / £2.70
Flat white £2.40 / £2.70

MAP REF.

 COFFEE 4.25 / 5  OVERALL 4.00 / 5 ★★★★☆

54

Caravan King's Cross

1 Granary Square, N1C 4AA

Inhabiting a monolithic former granary building, Caravan has graduated to the major league in both London's coffee and casual dining arenas. The unabashed use of concrete, and other reclaimed materials create an industrial atmosphere on a grand scale. The knowledgeable baristas are happy to offer advice on their seasonal blends, which are freshly roasted on the premises. The worldly food menu and wide range of coffees offer an excellent opportunity to experiment with coffee and food pairings.

+44(0)20 7101 7661
www.caravankingscross.co.uk
⊖ King's Cross

Sister locations Exmouth Market

MON-TUE. 8:00am - 10:30pm
WED-THU. 8:00am - 11:00pm
FRI. 8:00am - 12:00am
SAT. 10:00am - 12:00am
SUN. 10:00am - 4:00pm

First opened 2012
Roaster Caravan
Machine La Marzocco Strada EP, 3 groups, La Marzocco Linea, 2 groups
Grinder Mazzer Robur E x4, Mahlkönig Tanzania

Espresso £2.00
Cappuccino £2.60
Latte £2.60
Flat white £2.60

MAP REF. **43**

COFFEE 4.75 / 5

OVERALL 4.75 / 5 ★★★★½

Coffee Circus Crouch End

136 Crouch Hill, N8 9DX

Located in Crouch Hill, where good coffee used to be hard to find, Coffee Circus is well worth the journey north. With its circus theme and vintage tearoom feel, this café offers a warm and friendly space in which to meet for coffee and cake, but its links to the Coffee Circus wagon and kiosk at Camden Market also give it urban London caché. Coffee Circus is now supplied by its own roastery operation, Bean Wanders. Customers can purchase beans directly from the café and have them ground to order.

+44(0)75 0755 1472
www.coffeecircus.co.uk
 Crouch Hill

Sister locations Grand Piano (Camden Lock Village) / Coffee Wagon (Camden Stables)

MON–FRI. 8:00am – 6:00pm
SAT–SUN. 9:00am – 6:00pm

First opened 2010
Roaster Bean Wanders
Machine La Marzocco FB/80, 3 groups
Grinder Anfim, Mahlkönig Vario, Ditting

Espresso £1.80
Cappuccino £2.50
Latte £2.50
Flat white £2.50

MAP REF. **44**

  COFFEE 4.25 / 5  **OVERALL** 4.25 / 5 ★★★★☆

The Coffee Works Project

96-98 Islington High Street, N1 8EG

NEW

The Coffee Works Project owner Peter Theoklitou comes from a family of chefs and it shows. This stunning venue offers top-quality coffee and a fine deli menu.

The centrepiece of the café is a beautiful Seattle-made Slayer espresso machine – the first of its kind in London. A variety of Has Bean seasonal roasts are available as espresso and on filter, complemented by a range of British cheeses and charcuterie. The Coffee Works Project is an ambitious new addition to the London coffee scene and a must-visit destination.

+44(0)20 7424 5020
www.coffeeworksproject.com
⊖ Angel

MON-FRI. 7:30am - 6:00pm
SAT. 9:00am - 6:00pm
SUN. 10:00am - 4:00pm

First opened 2012
Roaster Has Bean
Machine Slayer, 3 groups
Grinder Mazzer Robur E, Anfim, Mahlkönig Tanzania

Espresso £2.00
Cappuccino £2.50
Latte £2.50
Flat white £2.50

MAP REF. **45**

COFFEE 4.50 / 5 🫘🫘🫘🫘🫘 | **OVERALL** 4.50 / 5 ★★★★★

The Espresso Room

31-35 Great Ormond Street, WC1N 3HZ

The Espresso Room is a simple concept: take a tiny space, add a Synesso espresso machine, Mazzer grinder, Square Mile beans and staff who are passionate and knowledgeable, and the result is consistently excellent coffee. Space may be limited here, but the chic wooden decor is warm and stylish. This espresso bar is widely considered one of London's very best. Join the queue of hospital staff, lawyers, Lamb's Conduit fashionistas and local residents to discover why.

+44(0)7760 714 883
www.theespressoroom.com
⊖ Russell Square

MON-FRI. 7:30am - 5:00pm
SAT-SUN. Closed

First opened 2009
Roaster Square Mile Coffee Roasters, Round Hill Roastery
Machine Synesso Hydra, 2 groups
Grinder Mazzer Robur E, Mahlkönig Vario, Ceado E37

Espresso £1.80 / £2.20
Cappuccino £2.80 / £3.40
Latte £2.80 / £3.40
Flat white £2.80 / £3.40

MAP REF. **46**

  COFFEE 4.75 / 5 OVERALL 4.25 / 5 ★★★★

The Fields Beneath

52 Prince of Wales Road, NW5 3NL

NEW

Named after Gillian Tindall's 1977 historical study of Kentish Town, this small speciality coffee outpost has already rallied a loyal local following. Owner Gavin Fernback, (previously of The Sandwich and Spoon) has converted a light-flooded railway arch at Kentish Town West station into a small but attractive coffee bar. The rotating coffee menu showcases up and coming British microroasters including Round Hill and Extract Coffee.

+44(0)7912 435 754

Kentish Town West

MON–FRI. 7:30am - 5:00pm
SAT. 9:00am - 2:00pm
SUN. Closed

First opened 2012
Roaster Federation, Round Hill Roastery and others
Machine La Marzocco Linea PID, 2 groups
Grinder Anfim Super Caimano

Espresso £2.00
Cappuccino £2.30
Latte £2.30
Flat white £2.30

MAP REF. **47**

Fix

161 Whitecross Street, EC1Y 8JL

Discreetly occupying a former pub adjacent to the Whitecross St Market, Fix is a spacious and stylish place to drop in for a coffee and bite to eat. Fix serves a Climpson's blend custom-roasted to their exact specification. Big leather couches, well-chosen vintage furniture and quirky light fittings make this a comfortable and dynamic space in which to hang out. Creatives and visitors to the weekday Whitecross Street market keep Fix buzzing and make it a favourite destination for coffee lovers.

+44(0)20 7998 3878
www.fix-coffee.co.uk
⊖ Old Street / Barbican

Sister locations Fix 126

MON-FRI. 7:00am - 7:00pm
SAT. 8:00am - 7:00pm
SUN. 9:00am - 7:00pm

First opened 2009
Roaster Climpson & Sons bespoke blend
Machine La Marzocco Linea PID, 3 groups
Grinder Mazzer Robur E, Mazzer Super Jolly E

Espresso £1.50 / £1.80
Cappuccino £2.30 / £2.50
Latte £2.30 / £2.50
Flat white £2.30

MAP REF. **48**

 COFFEE 4.25 / 5    OVERALL 4.25 / 5 ★★★★✩

Free State Coffee

23 Southampton Row, WC1B 5HA

 NEW

Raising the banner for third wave coffee in Holborn, this new coffee bar is already in fine fettle, sporting seasoned baristas and a healthy dose of American-style hospitality. Opened by the team behind New Row Coffee, Free State builds on its coffee pedigree with a wider selection of Union roasts, including the dark 'Foundation' blend which works particularly well with milk. Customers with time to linger can opt for a single estate filter coffee served at the dedicated brew bar.

+44(0)20 7998 1017
⊖ Holborn

Sister locations New Row Coffee

MON-FRI. 7:30am - 7:00pm
SAT-SUN. 9:00am - 6:00pm

First opened 2013
Roaster Union Hand-Roasted
Machine La Marzocco Strada EP, 3 groups
Grinder Mazzer Robur E, Mazzer Super Jolly x3

Espresso £2.00
Cappuccino £2.40
Latte £2.50
Flat white £2.00

MAP REF. **49**

 COFFEE 4.25 / 5    OVERALL 4.25 / 5 ★★★★✩

Ginger & White Belsize Park

2 England's Lane, NW3 4TG

Photo courtesy of the venue

Larger than its sister shop in Hampstead, Ginger & White Belsize Park was something of a happy accident - owners Tonia, Nicholas and Emma simply couldn't resist the high-ceilinged, sun-drenched corner venue when it became available. The café's kitchen supplies food to all three Ginger & White stores. The large communal table is well-stocked with homemade peanut butter and preserves, while the cute upstairs area and outdoor tables are ideal spots to tuck into the moreish sandwiches and decadent cakes.

+44(0)20 7722 9944
www.gingerandwhite.com
Chalk Farm / Belsize Park

Sister locations Hampstead / Soho

MON-FRI. 7:30am - 5:30pm
SAT-SUN. 8:30am - 5:30pm

First opened 2012
Roaster Square Mile Coffee Roasters
Machine La Marzocco FB/80, 3 groups
Grinder Mazzer Robur E, Mazzer Mini

Espresso £2.00
Cappuccino £2.70
Latte £2.70
Flat white £2.70

MAP REF. **50**

 **COFFEE** 4.50 / 5

OVERALL 4.25 / 5 ★★★★☆

61

Ginger & White Hampstead

4a-5a Perrin's Court, NW3 1QS

This proudly British café wears its heart on its sleeve. A local gem that is ever-popular with the Hampstead community, Ginger & White serves well-crafted Square Mile coffee alongside modern British meals made using locally sourced produce. With the choice of a communal dining table, window seats or intimate leather sofas, this is a great place to enjoy a leisurely brunch.

+44(0)20 7431 9098
www.gingerandwhite.com
⊖ Hampstead

Sister locations Belsize Park / Soho

MON-FRI. 7:30am - 5:30pm
SAT-SUN. 8:30am - 5:30pm

First opened 2009
Roaster Square Mile Coffee Roasters
Machine La Marzocco FB/80, 3 groups
Grinder Anfim, Mazzer Robur E

Espresso £2.00
Cappuccino £2.70
Latte £2.70
Flat white £2.70

MAP REF. **51**

COFFEE 4.50 / 5		OVERALL 4.25 / 5	★★★★☆

Harris + Hoole Crouch End

9 The Broadway, N8 8DU

 NEW

Harris + Hoole, named after two coffee loving characters featured in the diaries of Samuel Pepys, is a new breed of coffee bar bringing speciality coffee to the high street. The shabby chic interior is notable, and the Union coffee is undeniably excellent. Founded by the Tolley siblings (owners of Taylor St Baristas), Harris + Hoole draws on a high level of coffee expertise. With significant corporate backing, it is set to roll out additional stores across London and other parts of the UK.

www.harrisandhoole.co.uk
⊖ Crouch Hill

Sister locations Multiple locations throughout London

MON-FRI. 7:00am - 7:00pm
SAT. 8:30am - 7:00pm
SUN. 9:00am - 6:00pm

First opened 2012
Roaster Union Hand-Roasted bespoke blend
Machine Nuova Simonelli Aurelia II, 3 groups and 2 groups
Grinder Nuova Simonelli Mythos x4

Espresso £1.95
Cappuccino £2.30 / £2.60 / £3.00
Latte £2.30 / £2.60 / £3.00
Flat white £2.30 / £2.60 / £3.00

MAP REF. **52**

COFFEE 4.25 / 5		OVERALL 4.25 / 5	★★★★☆

Kipferl

20 Camden Passage, N1 8ED

Kipferl is a stylish venue offering the full traditional Viennese experience: coffee, cakes, strudel, soups, sausages and a full restaurant menu. The decor features muted grey, green and cream tones combined with timber panelling to create a warm, welcoming and peaceful space. Pop in for a melange and a rich Sachertorte for a real treat, or warm yourself with a gluhwein during the winter months.

+44(0)20 7704 1555
www.kipferl.co.uk
 Angel

Sister locations Kipferl Parkcafe Coram's Fields / Gordon Square

MON. Closed
TUE-SAT. 9:00am - 10:00pm
SUN. 10:00am - 10:00pm

First opened 2011
Roaster Helmut Sachers
Machine Gaggia, 2 groups
Grinder Mazzer Mini

Espresso £1.60 / £2.00
Cappuccino £2.60
Latte £2.90
Flat white £2.50 / £2.70

MAP REF. **53**

COFFEE 3.75 / 5 | **OVERALL** 4.00 / 5

Leyas

20 Camden High Street, NW1 0JH

Camden High Street has long been the domain of coffee chain outlets, but this independent provides a welcome alternative. Delicious Union coffee is served to take away or enjoy in the inviting downstairs area where customers lounge on mismatched vintage chairs and sofas. The café's walls are decorated by artworks and murals by local creatives. New this year are guest espresso blends rotated every few weeks. The cakes, made by a secret local supplier, are to die for.

www.leyas.co.uk
 Mornington Crescent

MON-FRI. 7:30am - 6:00pm
SAT-SUN. 9:30am - 6:00pm

First opened 2011
Roaster Union Hand-Roasted
Machine La Marzocco Linea, 2 groups
Grinder Mazzer Robur, Mazzer Super Jolly

Espresso £1.60
Cappuccino £2.20 / £2.50
Latte £2.20 / £2.50
Flat white £2.50

MAP REF. **54**

COFFEE 3.75 / 5 | **OVERALL** 4.00 / 5

Look Mum No Hands!

49 Old Street, EC1V 9HX

Look Mum No Hands! has rapidly become one of the city's busiest destinations for those who love bikes and coffee in equal measure. This lively café and bike workshop is decorated with bicycles, bike parts, and vintage cycling memorabilia. The outdoor area is now home to a coffee stall (a former RAF aircraft repair cart no less), which dispenses coffee to cyclists and pedestrians in a rush. A new range of British beers is available, and during the Tour de France, this place is a full-on party zone. If you love bikes, coffee or both, Look Mum No Hands! is an essential destination.

+44(0)20 7253 1025
www.lookmumnohands.com
⊖ Old Street / Barbican

MON-FRI. 7:00am – 10:00pm
SAT. 9:00am – 10:00pm
SUN. 10:00am – 10:00pm

First opened 2010
Roaster Square Mile Coffee Roasters
Machine Kees Van Der Westen Mirage, 2 groups, La Marzocco Linea, 2 groups
Grinder Anfim x3, Mazzer

Espresso £2.00
Cappuccino £2.80
Latte £2.80
Flat white £2.60

MAP REF. 55

 COFFEE 4.50 / 5    **OVERALL** 4.50 / 5

Maison d'Etre Coffee House

154 Canonbury Road, N1 2UP

This café on the Highbury roundabout is a labour of love for owners Kim and Kostas, who gave up their day jobs in 2010 to pursue a passion for food and coffee. Maison d'Etre serves Nude Espresso and a range of homemade cakes, sandwiches, treats and weekend brunch to an enthusiastic local crowd. Hand-painted murals, vintage china and a welcoming interior make this a serene spot to take five, particularly in summer in the back garden terrace.

+44(0)20 7226 4711
www.maisondetrecafe.co.uk
⊖ Highbury & Islington

MON-FRI. 7:30am - 6:00pm
SAT-SUN. 9:00am - 6:00pm

First opened 2011
Roaster Nude Espresso
Machine La Marzocco Linea, 2 group
Grinder Mazzer Super Jolly

Espresso £2.00
Cappuccino £2.20
Latte £2.20
Flat white £2.20

MAP REF. **56**

COFFEE 4.25 / 5		OVERALL 4.00 / 5	★★★★☆

Melrose and Morgan Primrose Hill

42 Gloucester Avenue, NW1 8JD

This grocer and deli in leafy Primrose Hill is a cornucopia of beautifully prepared, locally sourced food. Homemade preserves fill the shelves, alongside a daily selection of seasonal salads, sandwiches, soups, cakes and treats. Breads and vegetables are also available, together with artisanal foods and a range of gourmet readymade meals. The coffee is now of a very good standard, and Climpson's beans are available to purchase.

+44(0)20 7722 0011
www.melroseandmorgan.com
⊖ Chalk Farm / Camden Town

Sister locations Hampstead

MON-FRI. 8:00am - 7:00pm
SAT. 8:00am - 6:00pm
SUN. 9:00am - 5:00pm

First opened 2004
Roaster Climpson & Sons
Machine La Marzocco Linea, 2 groups
Grinder Anfim

Espresso £1.60 / £1.85
Cappuccino £2.40
Latte £2.40
Flat white £2.40

MAP REF. **57**

COFFEE 4.25 / 5		OVERALL 4.00 / 5	★★★★☆

Ottolenghi Islington

287 Upper Street, N1 2TZ

The outstanding food presentation at Ottolenghi makes this venue a feast for the eyes, as well as the taste buds. Piles of giant meringues, stacks of cakes, trays of fresh salads and an array of savouries create an irresistible display at the front of this well-known eatery. Communal tables and sleek, modern design helps keep Ottolenghi busy from morning until evening. Square Mile coffee makes the perfect digestif at the conclusion of a memorable brunch, lunch or dinner.

+44(0)20 7288 1454
www.ottolenghi.co.uk
⊖ Highbury & Islington /
⇝ Essex Road Rail

Sister locations Notting Hill / Kensington / Belgravia

MON–SAT. 8:00am – 11:00pm
SUN. 9:00am – 7:00pm

First opened 2004
Roaster Square Mile Coffee Roasters
Machine La Marzocco Linea, 2 groups
Grinder Mazzer

Espresso £1.95
Cappuccino £2.50 / £3.00
Latte £2.50 / £3.00
Flat white £2.50

MAP REF.

  COFFEE 4.00 / 5  OVERALL 4.50 / 5 ★★★★⯪

Salt

34 Great Queen Street, WC2B 5AA

 NEW

Salt's philosophy is "an honest but extreme view to ingredients", which means only the very best will do, from the coffee to the food, which is prepared on site by chefs. Lunches here are delicious, generous and extremely well priced, while the excellent coffees and teas are brewed to exacting standards by skilled baristas. The space is small but light and appealing, and a Victorian safe that was unearthed during renovations sits behind the counter, waiting to have its secrets unlocked.

+44(0)20 7430 0335
www.saltwc2.co.uk
⊖ Holborn

MON–FRI. 7:30am – 7:30pm
SAT. 10:00am – 7:30pm
SUN. Closed

First opened 2011
Roaster Square Mile Coffee Roasters
Machine La Marzocco FB/80, 3 groups
Grinder Mazzer Robur E, Mazzer Mini

Espresso £2.10
Cappuccino £2.50
Latte £2.60
Flat white £2.50

MAP REF.

 COFFEE 4.25 / 5  OVERALL 4.25 / 5 ★★★★⯪

Timberyard

61-67 Old Street, EC1V 9HW

Neither rough-hewn nor rustic, as its name might suggest, Timberyard is a slick yet friendly operation with big ambitions. The large tables and comfy seating downstairs make the space perfect for work or business meetings. iPads pre-loaded with subscriptions to popular news sites are also available to use. Timberyard offers some excellent coffee options, including Has Bean's citrusy 'Jabberwocky' blend. Single estate coffees brewed by 2-cup Chemex are ideal to share with a coffee-loving friend.

+44(0)20 3217 2009
www.timberyardlondon.com
Old Street / Barbican

MON-FRI. 8:00am - 8:00pm
SAT-SUN. 10:00am - 6:00pm

First opened 2012
Roaster Has Bean
Machine La Marzocco FB/80, 3 groups
Grinder Mazzer Robur E, Anfim

Espresso £1.80
Cappuccino £2.40
Latte £2.40
Flat white £2.30

MAP REF.

Tinderbox N1 Centre

N1 Centre, Parkfield Street, N1 0PS

Deceptively small on the ground floor, Tinderbox has much more to offer than may be apparent at first glance. The downstairs espresso bar is for takeaway only, so head up the wooden staircase to discover a large café with plenty of seating. Prized spots are the warm booths where customers can enjoy a Matthew Algie coffee or meet friends before seeing a film at the nearby cinema. Family-owned Tinderbox combines the professionalism of a small chain with the personal touch of an independent.

+44(0)20 7354 8929
⊖ Angel

Sister locations Spitalfields / Tottenham Court Road

MON-FRI. 6:30am - 10:30pm
SAT-SUN. 8:00am - 10:30pm

First opened 2009
Roaster Matthew Algie
Machine Elektra Barlume, 3 groups
Grinder Mazzer x2

Espresso £1.80 / £2.20
Cappuccino £2.10 / £2.50 / £2.90
Latte £2.50 / £2.90
Flat white £2.50

MAP REF. **61**

 COFFEE 4.00 / 5   **OVERALL** 4.00 / 5

Vagabond Stroud Green Road

Charter Court, Stroud Green Road N4 3SG

Vagabond adopts a wandering, nomadic approach to its coffee; Has Bean blends provide a top-quality base for a menu of beans sourced from roasters all over the world. Guest espressos and filter coffees vary frequently and offer a taste of the exotic in the otherwise sleepy suburban hamlet of Crouch Hill. A team of extremely friendly and passionate baristas man the coffee bar and bus a small number of tables both indoors and out.

+44(0)20 8616 4514
www.vagabondn4.co.uk
⊖ Finsbury Park / Crouch Hill

Sister locations Holloway Road

MON-SUN. 7:00am - 7:00pm

First opened 2012
Roaster Has Bean
Machine Nuova Simonelli Aurelia II, 3 groups
Grinder Mazzer, Mahlkönig Vario

Espresso £1.60
Cappuccino £2.30
Latte £2.30
Flat white £2.30

MAP REF. **62**

COFFEE 4.50 / 5		OVERALL 4.00 / 5	

Wild & Wood Coffee

1 New Oxford Street, WC1A 1BA

Wild & Wood's small interior has a warm and cosy feel, with wood panelling throughout, old church pew seats and an intimate seating nook. Classic photographs of beloved British TV characters and old-school rock 'n' roll music add to the authentic charm of this popular café, and Monmouth coffee is served on a La Marzocco Linea at some of the most reasonable prices in town.

+44(0)7525 155 957
www.wildandwoodcoffee.co.uk
⊖ Holborn / Tottenham Court Road

MON-FRI. 7:30am - 5:45pm
SAT. 10:00am - 5:30pm
SUN. 10:00am - 3:00pm

First opened 2008
Roaster Monmouth Coffee Company
Machine La Marzocco Linea, 2 groups
Grinder Mazzer Super Jolly

Espresso £1.30
Cappuccino £2.20
Latte £2.20
Flat white £2.20

MAP REF. **63**

COFFEE 4.00 / 5		OVERALL 4.00 / 5	

Carts & Kiosks

From neighbourhood farmers' markets to secluded city parks, London's coffee carts and kiosks caffeinate some of London's most captivating urban locations. Serving up coffee goodness in all weathers, these brave baristas are true heroes of the trade. Take the time to seek them out, and you'll soon discover a cadre of coffeeheads with fascinating stories to tell.

Bean About Town

Kentish Town Station, NW5 2AA

Bean About Town vans are a fixture on the streets of London, with six different outlets positioned at various points around town from Dalston to Clapham. The Kentish Town outlet has been doing business since 2005 and is a trusted favourite with locals and commuters seeking a quality caffeine hit. The Bean About Town ethos is all about quality and the personal touch, with well-trained baristas using lever machines to pull high-quality espresso for their loyal local customers.

+44(0)20 3239 6432
www.beanabouttown.com
Kentish Town

Sister locations Kensington Olympia /
St. Katharine Dock / Dalston Kingsland /
Clapham North / South Bank

MON-FRI. 7:00am – 4:30pm
SAT-SUN. 8:30am – 4:30pm

First opened 2005
Roaster Richard Jansz
Machine Izzo Pompei Lever, 2 groups
Grinder Mazzer Super Jolly

Espresso £1.30 / £1.60
Cappuccino £1.80 / £2.20 / £2.50
Latte £1.80 / £2.20 / £2.50
Flat white £1.80 / £2.20

MAP REF.

Blooming Good Coffee

Ezra Street, E2 7RH

Few places in London match Columbia Road Market on Sundays for sheer sensory delight. The flower stalls are a riot of hues, the atmosphere alive with colourful market patter, and the air perfumed by hundreds of bobbing bouquets. Blooming Good Coffee adds the fruity notes of Square Mile espresso to the heady mix. The cheerful baristas encourage customers to photograph themselves against this vibrant backdrop with disposable cameras loaned from the stall. The best shots are shared on their Facebook page.

⊖ Hoxton

SUN. 8:00am - 2:00pm
MON-SAT. Closed

First opened 2002
Roaster Square Mile Coffee Roasters
Machine La Marzocco Linea, 3 groups
Grinder Anfim

Espresso £1.90
Cappuccino £2.40
Latte £2.40
Flat white £2.40

MAP REF. **B**

Coleman Coffee

Unit 5, Dockley Road, SE16 3SF

Browsing the artisan food purveyors of Spa Terminus is a joy improved only by the addition of a cup of Coleman's coffee. Owner Jack Coleman has a refreshingly humble approach to his craft, and a clear affinity with machinery. A restored 1950s Viennese roaster (located in Camberwell) supplies a loyal circle of wholesale customers. The public can buy coffee and beans from the Saturdays-only stall. Pull up a crate, order a piccolo, and tuck into a pastry from neighbouring Little Bread Peddlar.

+44(0)7809 496 695
www.colemancoffee.com
⊖ Bermondsey

SAT. 8:30am - 2:00pm
SUN-FRI. Closed

First opened 2011
Roaster Coleman Coffee
Machine La Marzocco Linea, 2 groups
Grinder Mazzer Super Jolly

Espresso £1.50
Cappuccino £2.30
Latte £2.30
Flat white £2.30

MAP REF. **C**

Carts & Kiosks

Craft Coffee

The Ropewalk, Maltby Street Market, SE1 3PA

Splintering away from touristy Borough Market, the thriving set of artisan traders who line Maltby Street on Saturdays are passionate about their produce. Newcomer Craft Coffee (formerly Coffee, Mate?) displays incredible commitment to coffee excellence, rain or shine. Coffee is dosed carefully and extracted with precision on a Nuova Simonelli Appia. Craft's attention to detail puts many bricks and mortar cafés to shame. With expansion plans afoot, this is an outfit to keep an eye on.

Bermondsey / London Bridge

SAT. 9:00am – 3:00pm
SUN–FRI. Closed

First opened 2012
Roaster Has Bean
Machine Nuova Simonelli Appia, 2 groups
Grinder Mazzer Robur E, Mahlkönig Tanzania

Espresso £2.00
Cappuccino £2.40
Latte £2.60
Flat white £2.40

MAP REF. **D**

Dark Fluid

Brockley Market, Lewisham College Car Park, Lewisham Way, SE4 1UT

Dark Fluid has flourished into an award-winning boutique roastery and coffee vendor at Brockley Market. South London locals flock here on Saturdays for espresso blends and single origin beans hand roasted by passionate coffeehead Lawrence Sinclair. The growing number of local independent cafés now serving Dark Fluid is a testament to its success. Brockley Market is a destination in itself, with artisan producers offering a smorgasbord of fine foods, accompanied by several stalls serving hot fare.

+44(0)7984 886 723
www.darkfluid.co.uk
Brockley / St. John's Rail

SAT. 10:00am – 2:00pm
SUN–FRI. Closed

First opened 2011
Roaster Dark Fluid
Machine Izzo, 2 groups
Grinder Mazzer Major

Espresso £1.50
Cappuccino £2.50
Latte £2.50
Flat white £2.50

MAP REF. **E**

Flat Cap Coffee Co.

4 Strutton Ground, SW1P 2HR

The polished wagons of Flat Cap Coffee can be found dispensing fresh Square Mile espresso on weekdays at six locations throughout London. Owned by well-respected coffee barons Robert and Fabio of Notes, the Flat Cap carts are always a welcome sight around London and are synonymous with quality street coffee.

+44(0)7791 744 260
www.notes-uk.co.uk/flat-cap-carts
⊖ St James's Park

Sister locations Borough Market / St. Giles in the Fields / Fleet Street / Cannon Street / Aldgate

MON-FRI. 8:00am – 4:30pm
SAT-SUN. Closed

First opened 2009
Roaster Square Mile Coffee Roasters
Machine La Marzocco FB/80, 2 groups
Grinder Anfim Super Caimano

Espresso £1.00 / £1.50
Cappuccino £1.80 / £2.00
Latte £1.80 / £2.00
Flat white £1.80 / £2.50

MAP REF. **F**

Giddy Up

Fortune Street Park, EC1Y 0SB

Just around the corner from the famous Whitecross Street Market is Fortune Street Park, a charming patch of green in the backstreets of the Barbican that hosts one of the best coffee carts in London. Owner Lee Harte's barista street smarts were honed at the legendary Pitch 42, Columbia Road and Flat Cap coffee stalls. This expertise is evident in the attention to detail found here and at the three sister carts.

⊖ Moorgate / Old Street

Sister locations Guild Yard / Floripa / Angel

MON-FRI. 8:00am – 4:30pm
SAT-SUN. 10:00am – 4:00pm

First opened 2010
Roaster Square Mile Coffee Roasters, Has Bean
Machine La Marzocco GB/5, 2 groups
Grinder Anfim

Espresso £2.00
Cappuccino £2.60
Latte £2.60
Flat white £2.40

MAP REF. **G**

Merito Coffee

Swiss Cottage Farmers' Market, Eton Avenue, NW3 3EU

Bringing consistently excellent espresso to the markets of London since 2007, Merito Coffee is a welcome constant in an ever-changing London coffee landscape. Operating at the Swiss Cottage Market Tuesdays to Fridays, and the heaving Broadway Market on Saturdays, owner Jason Fitzpatrick and a crew of baristas use both an espresso machine and pour over filters to make some of London's best coffee for their loyal coterie of customers. Several varieties are also available for purchase.

+44(0)7703 121 579
www.meritocoffee.com
⊖ Swiss Cottage

Sister locations Broadway Market
(Saturdays)

TUE-FRI. 8:30am - 4:00pm
SAT-MON. Closed

First opened 2007
Roaster The Coffee Plant and various others
Machine Elektra, 2 groups
Grinder Mazzer Royal

Espresso £1.20 / £1.50
Cappuccino £1.80 / £2.00 / £2.30
Latte £1.80 / £2.00 / £2.30
Flat white £2.00 / £2.30

MAP REF.

Pitch 42

Whitecross Street Market, EC1Y 8JL

Pitch 42 occupies a place in London coffee history as a hotbed of coffee experimentation and espresso excellence, producing barista champions and a new generation of London coffee thought leaders. Under new ownership for a few years now, Pitch 42 is still a worthwhile coffee destination, not least for its location at the eclectic Whitecross Street lunchtime market.

+44(0)7534 883 477
⊖ Barbican / Old Street

MON-FRI. 7:00am - 3:00pm
SAT-SUN. Closed

First opened 2008
Roaster Square Mile Coffee Roasters
Machine Brugnetti, 2 groups
Grinder Mazzer Super Jolly

Espresso £1.60
Cappuccino £2.40
Latte £2.70
Flat white £2.10

MAP REF.

Terrone & Co.

Netil Market, 13-23 Westgate Street, E8 3RL

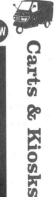

Carts & Kiosks

Located in Netil Market (near Broadway Market), Terrone is possibly the only Italian third wave producer based in London. Originally from Salerno, enthusiastic owner Edy bucks the trend of the conservative Italian coffee fraternity with his lighter-roasted blends. The high standard of Terrone's coffee has already garnered plaudits, winning a gold star in the 2012 UK Great Taste Awards. Make the trip on a Saturday morning and wake up to an expertly poured Bianco Piatto (the Italian flat white).

www.terrone.co.uk
⇌ London Fields Rail

SAT. 9:30am – 5:30pm
SUN-FRI. Closed

First opened 2012
Roaster Terrone & Co.
Machine La Marzocco GB/5, 2 groups
Grinder Anfim

Espresso £2.00
Cappuccino £2.60
Flat white £2.40

MAP REF.

UNION®

HAND-ROASTED COFFEE

 Union Direct Trade   **Artisan Roasted**   **Exquisite Coffee**

Directly sourcing exclusive microlots; small parcels of delicousness full of vibrant and exquisite flavours.
We are served by some of London's top baristas and are also available roast-to-order for brewing at home.

 Visit our website to buy online; **www.unionroasted.com**

 @unionroasted   /unionroasted

Inner East

Brick Lane and Shoreditch provide London's creative pulse and are areas of tremendous diversity that have undergone rapid change in recent years. Many of the city's best new roasteries are based in East London and a range of artisan coffee venues provide fuel for the artists, students and urbanites who flock here for the weekend markets.

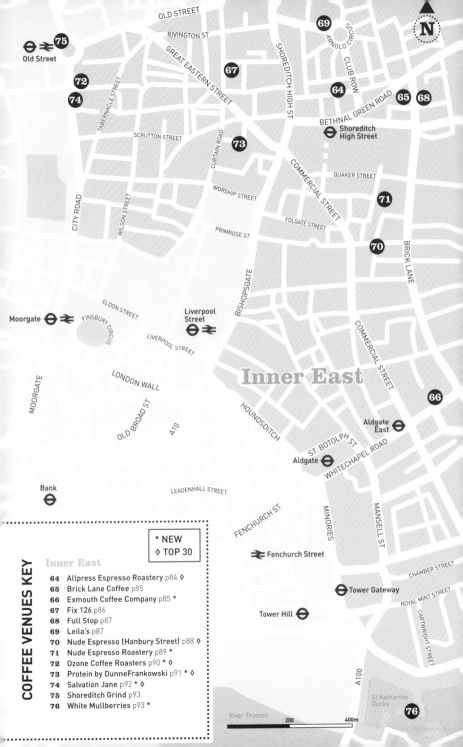

Allpress Espresso Roastery

58 Redchurch Street, E2 7DP

This first UK venue for well-established New Zealand roastery Allpress Espresso has rapidly become a firm favourite in the heart of Shoreditch. The café's simple, natural interior focuses attention on the coffee itself, and a gleaming roaster is proudly on display. Allpress has had huge success in New Zealand and Australia, and is continuing its winning run in the UK, supplying many high-quality coffee shops and restaurants. Allpress has thrown out a challenge to the UK market and coffee lovers are reaping the rewards.

+44(0)20 7749 1780
www.allpressespresso.com
⊖ Shoreditch High Street

MON-FRI. 8:00am - 5:00pm
SAT-SUN. 9:00am - 5:00pm

First opened 2010
Roaster Allpress Espresso
Machine La Marzocco Linea, 3 groups
Grinder Mazzer Robur, Mazzer Super Jolly, Mahlkönig

Espresso £2.00
Cappuccino £2.70
Latte £2.70
Flat white £2.70

MAP REF.

Brick Lane Coffee

157 Brick Lane, E1 6SB

Situated at the northern end of Brick Lane, the headquarters of the Street Coffee mini-chain oozes alternative cool. The mish-mash of vintage furniture, eclectic wall art featuring pop-culture icons and the bicycles crammed inside create a youthful, urban feel. Art students and East London locals linger on the couches, except on Sundays when Brick Lane Market turns this café into a heaving hub for bargain hunters. The smoothies and frappés are also popular here.

+44(0)20 7729 2667
www.streetcoffee.co.uk
 Shoreditch High Street

Sister locations Goswell Road / Bermondsey Street

MON-SUN. 7:00am - 8:00pm

First opened 2001
Roaster Brick Lane Coffee
Machine Rancilio Classe 8, 3 groups
Grinder Mazzer Robur, Mazzer Royal, Mazzer Mini

Espresso £1.70 / £1.50
Cappuccino £2.20 / £2.50 / £2.80
Latte £2.20 / £2.50 / £2.80
Flat white £2.30 / £2.50

MAP REF. **65**

COFFEE 4.25 / 5		OVERALL 4.25 / 5	

Exmouth Coffee Company

83 Whitechapel High Street, E1 7QX

 NEW

In a city now peppered with cool antipodean cafés, Exmouth offers a refreshingly eclectic mixture of East End and North African influences. Situated next to Whitechapel Gallery, this lively venue attracts a diverse, arty crowd. Roasted in-house, the coffee is dark and chocolatey, but without a hint of bitterness. Food is freshly prepared in front of customers, and extraordinarily presented. The flatbread sandwiches, quiches, and sinfully sticky pecan brownies will keep you coming back for more.

+44(0)20 7377 1010
 Aldgate East / Aldgate

Sister locations Pitfield

MON-SUN. 7:30am - 8:00pm

First opened 2012
Roaster Exmouth Coffee Company
Machine La Marzocco Linea, 3 groups
Grinder Mazzer Robur E, Mazzer Super Jolly E

Espresso £2.00
Cappuccino £2.70
Latte £2.70
Flat white £2.70

MAP REF. **66**

COFFEE 4.25 / 5		OVERALL 4.25 / 5	

Fix 126

126 Curtain Road, Shoreditch, EC2A 3PJ

This second Fix location in the heart of Shoreditch is a hub of creativity and a popular place for local creatives to meet and collaborate, or simply work alone on laptops or sketchbooks. This is also an excellent spot to stop for a daily caffeine fix, and friendly staff are happy to chat while whipping up a cup of custom-blended Climpson's espresso. A stool at one of the large front windows is the ideal place to sit and watch the comings and goings along vibrant Curtain Road.

+44(0)20 7033 9555
www.fix-coffee.co.uk
⊖ Old Street / Shoreditch High Street

Sister locations Fix (Whitecross Street)

MON–FRI. 7:00am – 7:00pm
SAT–SUN. 8:00am – 7:00pm

First opened 2011
Roaster Climpson & Sons bespoke blend
Machine La Marzocco GB/5, 3 groups
Grinder Mazzer Robur E, Mazzer Super Jolly E x2

Espresso £1.50 / £2.00
Cappuccino £2.40 / £2.60
Latte £2.40 / £2.60
Flat white £2.40

 COFFEE 4.25 / 5   OVERALL 4.00 / 5

Full Stop

202 Brick Lane, E1 6SA

Fittingly for its location, a vintage aesthetic predominates at Full Stop, with bench seats, Formica tables and comfy sofas furnishing a long, cosy space. However, the offering here is far from antique, with fresh gourmet sandwiches and cakes providing the perfect complement to expertly prepared Square Mile espresso. Visit in the evening for an interesting selection of beers, wines and ciders. Owner Peter Duggan's old Indie Coffee cart pops up occasionally, serving coffee on the street.

+44(0)20 7739 7086
⊖ Shoreditch High Street

MON-TUE. 7:30am – 9:30pm
WED-THU. 7:30am – 11:00pm
FRI. 7:30am – 12:30am
SAT. 9:00am – 12:30am
SUN. 9:00am – 9:30pm

First opened 2011
Roaster Square Mile Coffee Roasters
Machine La Marzocco Linea, 2 groups
Grinder Mazzer, Anfim

Espresso £2.00
Cappuccino £2.70
Latte £2.70
Flat white £2.70

MAP REF. **68**

  COFFEE **4.25 / 5**  OVERALL **4.00 / 5** ★★★★☆

Leila's

17 Calvert Avenue, E2 7JP

Leila's combines a country kitchen with a local café to create one of Shoreditch's cosiest and most appealing venues. The Leila's Shop deli (next door to the café) sells a wide range of produce from fruit and veg to preserves and pasta. The café offers simple but beautifully prepared breakfasts and lunches to East Londoners looking for something more authentic than the usual painfully hip fare. Like the food, the coffee is prepared with care to a high standard.

+44(0)20 7729 9789
⊖ Shoreditch High Street

MON-TUE. Closed
WED-SAT. 10:00am – 6:00pm
SUN. 10:00am – 5:00pm

First opened 2002
Roaster Coleman Coffee
Machine La Marzocco Linea, 2 groups
Grinder Mazzer

Espresso £2.00
Cappuccino £2.50 / £2.80
Latte £2.50 / £2.80
Flat white £2.50 / £2.80

MAP REF. **69**

COFFEE **4.00 / 5**  OVERALL **4.00 / 5** ★★★★☆

Nude Espresso Hanbury Street

26 Hanbury Street, E1 6QR

Located close to the bustling Spitalfields and Brick Lane markets, Nude Espresso is one of London's busiest weekend destinations for food and coffee lovers. Nude offers much more than just a pit stop for weekend shoppers, with its famous 'East' espresso blend and filter options making it well worth braving the mobs any day of the week. The Nude Espresso Roastery itself is just around the corner on Brick Lane, for anyone who is interested to learn more about the coffee-making process.

+44(0)7712 899 335
www.nudeespresso.com
⊖ Shoreditch High Street / Liverpool Street

Sister locations Soho / Nude Roastery
(Old Truman Brewery)

MON–FRI. 7:00am – 7:00pm
SAT–SUN. 9:30am – 7:00pm

First opened 2008
Roaster Nude Coffee Roasters
Machine La Marzocco FB/80, 3 groups
Grinder Compak K-10 x3

Espresso £2.00
Cappuccino £2.80
Latte £2.80
Flat white £2.80

MAP REF. 70

COFFEE 4.75 / 5    **OVERALL** 4.50 / 5 ★★★★½

Nude Espresso Roastery

The Cooperage Yard, Old Truman Brewery, 91-95 Brick Lane, E1 6QL

NEW

The Nude Espresso Roastery relocated to these premises after outgrowing its home at the Hanbury Street café. Just a short walk away on Brick Lane, this fresh and inviting space is where it all happens. Beans are roasted in small batches on a 15kg Toper roaster, keeping Nude's three venues and a growing list of independent coffee bars well supplied. Visit to learn about the process of coffee selection, roasting and tasting from those who know it best, or simply to enjoy a coffee in an unusual space.

+44(0)7804 223 590
www.nudeespresso.com
⊖ Shoreditch High Street / Liverpool Street

Sister locations Soho / Hanbury Street

MON-FRI. 8:30am - 5:00pm
SAT-SUN. Closed

First opened 2008
Roaster Nude Coffee Roasters
Machine La Marzocco FB/80, 3 groups
Grinder Compak K-10 x3

Espresso £2.00
Cappuccino £2.80
Latte £2.80
Flat white £2.80

MAP REF. **71**

COFFEE 4.50 / 5

OVERALL 4.25 / 5 ★★★★☆

Ozone Coffee Roasters

11 Leonard Street, EC2A 4AQ

NEW

Three years in the making, this huge dual-level roastery, café and bar is a stunning addition to London's coffee scene. A central island on the first floor contains an open kitchen, around which are arrayed bar stools where customers can sip a brew and watch their food being prepared. Further seating is provided downstairs, in view of the magnificent Probat roaster. Ozone's decor is a combination of Victorian industrial, Kiwi kitsch and South American barrio, resulting in a contemporary yet welcoming atmosphere that exudes an overarching passion for coffee.

+44(0)20 7490 1039
www.ozonecoffee.co.uk
⊖ Old Street

MON-FRI. 7:30am - 5:00pm
SAT-SUN. 9:00am - 4:00pm

First opened 2012
Roaster Ozone Coffee Roasters
Machine Synesso Hydra, 3 groups and Nuova Simonelli Aurelia T3, 3 groups
Grinder Mazzer Robur E x2, Mazzer Super Jolly, Mahlkönig

Espresso £1.80
Cappuccino £2.40
Latte £2.40
Flat white £2.40

MAP REF. **72**

 COFFEE 4.75 / 5

 OVERALL 4.75 / 5 ★★★★★

Protein by DunneFrankowski

18 Hewett Street, EC2A 3NN

Coffee cognoscenti Rob Dunne and Victor Frankowski have made a significant contribution to London's progressive coffee scene as educators and creatives as well as baristas. Their stripped-back coffee bar, residing in the 18 Hewett Street gallery space, takes the coffee experience back to its essentials. The absence of a menu encourages customers to converse with the baristas to explore their preferences. The rotating coffee offer showcases an exotic assortment of beans from some of the world's finest microroasters. Those keen to further their knowledge and skills can sign up for DunneFrankowski's weekend coffee workshops.

www.dunnefrankowski.com
⊖ Shoreditch High Street

MON-FRI. 8:00am - 5:00pm
SAT-SUN. Closed

First opened 2011
Roaster Workshop Coffee Co., Square Mile Coffee Roasters and others
Machine La Cimbali M39, 2 groups
Grinder Anfim, Mahlkönig Tanzania

Espresso £1.50
Cappuccino £2.50
Latte £2.50
Flat white £2.50

MAP REF. **73**

COFFEE 4.75 / 5   🫘🫘🫘🫘🫘

OVERALL 4.25 / 5   ★★★★⯪

Salvation Jane

1 Oliver's Yard, 55 City Road, EC1Y 1HQ

Salvation Jane takes its name from a beautiful flower that thrives in the Australian desert. This antipodean newcomer has helped transform East London's once arid coffee landscape into a blossoming caffeine community. A takeout bar serves those in a rush, and the large mid-century-inspired casual dining room is a fashionable spot for evening meals with cocktails. Salvation Jane's formidable brunch menu and potent Square Mile coffee are more than a match for even the most grievous Shoreditch hangover.

+44(0)20 7253 5273
www.salvationjanecafe.co.uk
⊖ Old Street

Sister locations Lantana

MON. 7:30am – 4:00pm
TUE-FRI. 7:30am – 11:00pm
SAT-SUN. 9:00am – 4:00pm

First opened 2012
Roaster Square Mile Coffee Roasters
Machine La Marzocco FB/80, La Marzocco Linea
Grinder Mazzer Robur E

Espresso £1.80 / £2.00
Cappuccino £2.60
Latte £2.60
Flat white £2.60

MAP REF. **74**

COFFEE 4.50 / 5

OVERALL 4.50 / 5

Shoreditch Grind

213 Old Street, EC1V 9NR

With its retro cinema signage, circular interior and prime location right on the Old Street 'Silicon' roundabout, Shoreditch Grind is coffee theatre at its finest. Coffee lovers can sit on bar stools and look out at one of the city's busiest transport hubs while feeling insulated from the rat race with a cup of the delicious house blend in hand. A recording studio upstairs is available for local musicians to hire. As the Shoreditch night draws in, the café transforms into a hip bar serving beers, wines and cocktails.

+44(0)20 7490 7490
www.shoreditchgrind.com
 Old Street (Exit 8)

MON-THU. 7:00am - 11:00pm
FRI. 7:00am - 1:00am
SAT. 8:00am - 1:00am
SUN. 9:00am - 6:00pm

First opened 2011
Roaster Shoreditch Grind House
Espresso Blend
Machine La Marzocco Linea, 2 Groups x2
Grinder Mazzer

Espresso £2.10
Cappuccino £2.65 / £2.95
Latte £2.65 / £2.95
Flat white £2.65 / £2.95

MAP REF. **75**

 COFFEE 4.50 / 5    **OVERALL 4.50 / 5** ★★★★⯨

White Mulberries

D3 Ivory House, St Katharine Docks, E1W 1AT

 NEW

Like its namesake, White Mulberries is a sweet find; a rare combination of beautiful setting and great coffee. Located in St Katharine Docks - London's little-known marina - visitors have an enviable view of the swan-like sailboats. The café really comes into its own in fine weather when outdoor seating is provided overlooking the water. Customers have the option of Allpress Espresso, or single origin coffee brewed by AeroPress. Accompany your coffee with an award winning 'super moist' brownie.

www.whitemulberries.com
 Tower Hill / Tower Gateway DLR

MON-FRI. 7:00am - 5:00pm
SAT. 8:00am - 5:00pm
SUN. 9:00am - 5:00pm

First opened 2012
Roaster Allpress Espresso
Machine La Marzocco Linea, 2 groups
Grinder Mazzer Major

Espresso £1.90
Cappuccino £2.30 / £2.60
Latte £2.30 / £2.60
Flat white £2.30 / £2.60

MAP REF. **76**

 COFFEE 4.25 / 5    **OVERALL 4.25 / 5** ★★★★⯨

Hackney

Hackney has successfully shaken off its label as a rough outer region to emerge as London's booming artistic neighbourhood. A wonderful combination of cultures and a thriving creative scene have helped put Hackney back on the map, and provide a fertile environment for London's coffee pioneers.

46b Espresso Hut

46b Brooksby's Walk, E9 6DA

Photo courtesy of the venue

Locals should seriously consider altering their morning commute expressly to visit 46b. Visitors from elsewhere will discover some of the best coffee served in Hackney in this unassuming, yet enchanting café. It's all espresso-based for now, but the zesty Red Brick blend pulled through the Seattle-made Synesso Cyncra is worth travelling for. Scrupulously selected suppliers include Northiam Dairy, E5 Bakehouse, and London Borough of Jam. 46b is without doubt this year's quietly brilliant new venue.

+44(0)77 0206 3172
www.46b-espressohut.co.uk
⊖ Homerton

MON-FRI. 7:30am - 6:30pm
SAT. 9:00am - 6:30pm
SUN. 10:00am - 6:00pm

First opened 2012
Roaster Square Mile Coffee Roasters
Machine Synesso Cyncra, 2 groups
Grinder Anfim Super Caimano and Mazzer

Espresso £1.90
Cappuccino £2.20
Latte £2.20
Flat white £2.20

MAP REF. 77

COFFEE 4.50 / 5		OVERALL 4.25 / 5	★ ★ ★ ★ ☆

Cà Phê VN (Saigon Street Cafe)

Broadway Market, E8 4PH

Occupying a stall in Broadway Market every Saturday, Cà Phê VN provides a Vietnamese-style caffeine hit like no other in London. Strong filter coffee is made using a traditional phin and optionally sweetened with condensed milk. Relax in a canvas deck chair and enjoy a heart-starting iced coffee (their summer specialty) as the eclectic market crowd strolls by. Husband-and-wife team Rob Atthill and Tuyen Hong source their coffee directly from farmers in Vietnam, and also supply to several restaurants.

+44(0)7780 784 696
www.caphevn.co.uk
⊖ Haggerston /
⇌ Cambridge Heath Rail

Sister locations Pho Express (Islington)

SAT. 10:00am - 5:00pm
SUN-FRI. Closed

First opened 2007
Roaster Cà Phê VN
Machine Vietnamese phin

Filter £1.50
Iced coffee £2.00

MAP REF. **78**

    COFFEE 4.00 / 5

 OVERALL 3.75 / 5

Hackney

Climpson & Sons

67 Broadway Market, E8 4PH

Revered by coffee lovers in East London and beyond, the Climpson & Sons café and roastery has developed into one of the biggest names in London coffee. You'll be lucky to even make it through the door of the café while Broadway Market is in full swing on Saturdays, and the seats outside are often packed. Luckily the team operates a stall at the southern end of the market to help meet demand. Their roastery is located just up the road and supplies a growing number of London's best cafés and restaurants.

+44(0)20 7812 9829
www.climpsonandsons.com
Haggerston / Cambridge Heath Rail

Sister locations Climpson & Sons Broadway Market Stall (Saturdays only)

MON-FRI. 7:30am - 5:00pm
SAT. 8:30am - 5:00pm
SUN. 9:00am - 5:00pm

First opened 2004
Roaster Climpson & Sons
Machine La Marzocco FB/80, 3 groups
Grinder Mazzer Robur x2, Mazzer Super Jolly x2

Espresso £1.60
Cappuccino £2.20 / £2.40
Latte £2.20 / £2.40
Flat white £2.20 / £2.40

MAP REF. **79**

 COFFEE 4.50 / 5  **OVERALL** 4.50 / 5

Cooper & Wolf

145 Chatsworth Road E5 0LA

Occupying a sunny spot on gentrifying Chatsworth Road, Cooper & Wolf's Swedish charm is irresistible. Curious Scandinavian ornaments peep out from between plant pots, and lilting Nordic accents punctuate the atmosphere. Caravan coffee is exquisitely served by Alex and his baristas, while his wife and co-owner Sara heads up a kitchen offering delicious Swedish fare, many from old family recipes. The råraka with Hansen & Lydersen salmon makes a particularly delicious accompaniment to a morning cappuccino.

www.cooperandwolf.co.uk
 Homerton / Clapton Rail

MON-THU. 9:00am - 5:30pm
FRI. 9:00am - 6:00pm
SAT-SUN. 10:00am - 6:00pm

First opened 2012
Roaster Caravan
Machine Synesso Cyncra, 2 groups
Grinder Mazzer Super Jolly, Anfim

Espresso £1.60
Cappuccino £2.40
Latte £2.40
Flat white £2.40

MAP REF. 80

COFFEE 4.25 / 5		OVERALL 4.25 / 5	★★★★

The Counter Café

Stour Space, 7 Roach Road, E3 2PA

The Counter Café occupies an area within Hackney Wick's Stour Space gallery, with a gorgeous view directly onto the canal. With smashed brick walls and signature vintage cinema seats, the interior has a grungy charm. The expanded menu means difficult decisions at ordering time and the Square Mile coffee remains excellent. The café's nearby sister business, Crate Brewery, keeps the local artists well supplied with craft beer and pizza. The Counter Café is a thriving venue well worth the journey.

+44(0)7834 275 920
www.thecountercafe.co.uk
 Hackney Wick

MON-FRI. 7:45am - 5:00pm
SAT-SUN. 9:00am - 5:00pm

First opened 2009
Roaster Square Mile Coffee Roasters
Machine Synesso Cyncra, 2 groups
Grinder Anfim

Espresso £1.50
Cappuccino £2.20
Latte £2.50
Flat white £2.20

MAP REF. 81

COFFEE 4.25 / 5	OVERALL 4.50 / 5	★★★★

E5 Bakehouse

Arch 395, Mentmore Terrace, E8 3PH

This busy bakery churns out hundreds of organic loaves of bread every day, as well as serving great coffee. With huge bags of flour stacked on the rough floorboards and the enticing smell of baking bread filling the cavernous space, visiting E5 Bakehouse is more like walking into an old-fashioned mill than an urban café. During the week, locals stop by for a chat, to read the papers or to grab their daily loaf, but on Saturdays, they queue out the door for fresh bread and bagels. Baking classes are also popular.

+44(0)7548 300 244
www.e5bakehouse.com
London Fields Rail

MON-SUN. 7:00am - 7:00pm

SOYA

First opened 2010
Roaster Nude Espresso
Machine Wega, 2 groups
Grinder Mazzer Super Jolly

Espresso £1.50
Cappuccino £2.20
Latte £2.20
Flat white £2.20

MAP REF. 82

COFFEE 3.75 / 5

OVERALL 4.00 / 5

Embassy East

285 Hoxton Street, N1 5JX

NEW

Behind the plain exterior and nondescript street address, Embassy East is a café with real soul. Opened on a modest budget, the visitor soon senses the love and ingenuity invested by the three founding friends (formerly of Flat White). It's the small things that make this Hoxton coffee bar special: the cleverly modified grinder, quirky pickle jar light fittings, and nostalgic cartons of Kellogg's cereal. The open kitchen also offers carefully prepared food made fresh with artisanal ingredients.

+44(0)20 7739 8340
www.embassyeast.co.uk
Hoxton

MON-FRI. 8:00am - 6:00pm
SAT-SUN. 10:00am - 6:00pm

SOYA

First opened 2013
Roaster Workshop Coffee Co.
Machine La Marzocco Linea, 3 groups
Grinder Modified Anfim, Mahlkönig Columbia

Espresso £2.00
Cappuccino £2.50
Latte £2.70
Flat white £2.20

MAP REF. 83

COFFEE 4.50 / 5

OVERALL 4.25 / 5

Fabrica 584

584 Kingsland Road, Dalston, E8 4AH

Fabrica's owners Roberto and George are Italian and Greek respectively, and their Mediterranean sensibilities combine to make this café a satisfying alternative to the usual laidback style of Kiwi and Aussie-owned coffee bars. The industrial interior furnished with mismatched tables and chairs gives way to a gorgeous outdoor area and, in a pleasing twist, coffee and tea arrive in glass cups and saucers, while water and juice are served in jars.

+44(0)20 7998 8041
⊖ Dalston Junction

MON-FRI. 8:30am - 7:00pm
SAT. 9:30am - 7:00pm
SUN. 10:00am - 6:00pm

First opened 2011
Roaster Monmouth Coffee Company
Machine Faema E61, 2 groups
Grinder Mazzer Super Jolly

Espresso £1.50
Cappuccino £2.30
Latte £2.30
Flat white £2.50

MAP REF. **84**

Fred & Fran

55 Kynaston Road, N16 0EB

Tucked away on one of Stoke Newington's back streets is Fred & Fran, a warm and welcoming café filled with the aroma of fresh baking. Owner Demelza Donohoo named Fred & Fran after her grandparents and applies to her charming venue the sort of care and attention to detail that was more typical of that generation. The beautiful Scandinavian-style interior is stylish and comfortable with blonde wood fittings and sleek, contemporary furniture.

+44(0)20 7254 0253
www.fredandfran.com
≥ Rectory Road Rail / Stoke Newington Rail

MON–FRI. 8:30am – 5:00pm
SAT. 9:00am – 5:00pm
SUN. 10:00am – 4:00pm

First opened 2011
Roaster Square Mile Coffee Roasters
Machine La Marzocco Linea, 2 groups
Grinder Anfim

Espresso £2.00
Cappuccino £2.60
Latte £2.60
Flat white £2.40

MAP REF. **85**

  **COFFEE** 4.25 / 5 **OVERALL** 4.25 / 5

Grind Coffee Bar Westfield Stratford City

Lower ground floor, Westfield Stratford, E20 1EJ

A vast shopping mall is the last place you'd expect to find great coffee, but tucked away down one end of Westfield Stratford is an outpost of Putney café Grind. The venue occupies a large, open-plan space designed to provide a respite from the bedlam of the shopping mall, with kitchen-style tables, leather wingback chairs and a soothing New Zealand theme. Coffee is tailored for busy shoppers but more serious options are also available in the form of guest espresso and single-origin filters.

www.grindcoffeebar.co.uk
⊖ Stratford

Sister locations Putney / Battersea

MON–FRI. 8:00am – 9:00pm
SAT. 9:00am – 9:00pm
SUN. 11:00am – 6:00pm

First opened 2011
Roaster London Coffee Roasters
Machine La Marzocco Strada EP, 3 groups
Grinder Mazzer Robur x2

Espresso £1.80
Cappuccino £2.30 / £2.70 / £2.90
Latte £2.30 / £2.70 / £2.90
Flat white £2.30 / £2.70 / 2.90

MAP REF. **86**

  COFFEE 4.25 / 5 **OVERALL** 4.00 / 5

The Hackney Pearl

11 Prince Edward Road, E9 5LX

Hidden away in the Hackney Wick industrial area, The Hackney Pearl rewards the urban explorer with simple, yet delicious coffee and food. The Pearl serves as a hub for the growing community of local artists, many of whom work in studios nearby. The broad glass shopfront admits plenty of natural light, and outdoor seating is also plentiful. The beautiful seasonal menu changes daily and an extensive bar list is also available. The Pearl is open until late every evening for dinner, drinks and events.

+44(0)20 8510 3605
www.thehackneypearl.com
⊖ Hackney Wick

MON-FRI. 8:00am – 11:00pm
SAT-SUN. 10:00am – 5:00pm

First opened 2009
Roaster Square Mile Coffee Roasters
Machine Gaggia D90, 3 groups
Grinder Mazzer Super Jolly

Espresso £1.70 / £2.10
Cappuccino £2.00 / £2.40
Latte £2.00 / £2.40
Flat white £2.00 / £2.40

MAP REF. **87**

COFFEE 4.00 / 5		OVERALL 4.00 / 5	

Haggerston Espresso Room

Unit C, 13 Downham Road, N1 5AA

 (NEW)

Haggerston Espresso Room, or HER as this Dalston darling likes to be known, is a sweetheart of the Hackney creative brigade. The mismatched furniture is a combination of school classroom and grandmother chic, which is sure to suit East End fashionistas down to the ground (quite literally; the sofas boast considerable sag). Fortunately the Climpson's coffee is no slouch, and 'sexy toast' contributes to a seductive food menu. HER is a characterful café with a sense of humour you can't help but like.

+44(0)20 7249 0880
⊖ Haggerston

MON-FRI. 7:30am – 6:00pm
SAT. 9:00am – 6:00pm
SUN. 10:00am – 6:00pm

First opened 2011
Roaster Climpson & Sons
Machine La Marzocco Linea, 3 groups
Grinder Mazzer Royal, Mazzer Super Jolly

Espresso £1.80 / £2.00
Cappuccino £2.50
Latte £2.40
Flat white £2.40

MAP REF. **88**

COFFEE 4.00 / 5		OVERALL 4.00 / 5	

Mouse & De Lotz

103 Shacklewell Lane, E8 2EB

To enter Mouse & De Lotz is to step back in time to an era of glass milk bottles, Singer sewing machines and cakes made by hand. Squashy sofas, window seats and a pretty, vintage aesthetic enhance the comforting retro feel, but free wifi brings this café right up to date and makes it an ideal place to spend a lazy hour. Superb coffee is prepared by a rotating staff of artists, students and parents, all of whom bring full-time passion to the food and drinks they prepare for their Dalston customers.

+44(0)20 3489 8082
www.mousedelotz.com
⊖ Dalston Kingsland

MON–FRI. 8:00am – 6:00pm
SAT. 9:00am – 6:00pm
SUN. 10:00am – 6:00pm

First opened 2010
Roaster Square Mile Coffee Roasters
Machine La Marzocco Linea, 2 groups
Grinder Anfim

Espresso £1.80
Cappuccino £2.20
Latte £2.20
Flat white £2.20

MAP REF.

 COFFEE 4.00 / 5   **OVERALL** 4.00 / 5 ★★★★☆

Railroad

120-122 Morning Lane, E9 6LH

A visit to Railroad is food for both the body and the mind - the delicious and inventive seasonal menu (produced as if by magic from a tiny kitchen) is complemented by a small range of books for sale. Square Mile coffee is served in handmade earthenware cups that lend themselves to being held in both hands on cold days. The café's sunny corner location makes it an ideal spot to sit and bask in the sunshine.

+44(0)20 8985 2858
www.railroadhackney.co.uk
⊖ Hackney Central / Homerton

MON-TUE. Closed
WED-FRI. 11:00am - 11:00pm
SAT. 10:00am - 11:00pm
SUN. 10:00am - 5:00pm

First opened 2010
Roaster Square Mile Coffee Roasters
Machine Nuova Simonelli, 2 groups
Grinder Anfim, Mazzer Mini

Espresso £1.50 / £1.90
Cappuccino £2.20 / £2.40
Latte £2.20 / £2.40
Flat white £2.20 / £2.40

MAP REF. **90**

 COFFEE 4.25 / 5  **OVERALL** 4.25 / 5 ★★★★⯪

Reilly Rocket

507 Kingsland Road, E8 4AU

Situated behind a motorcycle shop on Kingsland Road, Reilly Rocket is the antidote to twee, chintzy cafés and industrial chic. Decorated with colourful memorabilia, cactus plants, brown leather sofas, taxidermy and graphic wall art, Reilly's is a haven for lovers of rebellion and retro road culture. Hunter S. Thompson would have been right at home here, and a memorial to British racing legend Barry Sheene adorns one wall. The coffee is just as gutsy and is pulled by a committed team of hardcore baristas.

www.reillyrocket.com
⊖ Dalston Junction

MON-FRI. 8:00am - 5:00pm
SAT. 9:00am - 5:00pm
SUN. 10:00am - 5:00pm

First opened 2011
Roaster Square Mile Coffee Roasters
Machine La Marzocco Linea, 2 groups
Grinder Mazzer

Espresso £1.80
Cappuccino £2.40
Latte £2.40
Flat white £2.40

MAP REF. **91**

COFFEE 4.25 / 5

OVERALL 4.00 / 5

Tina, We Salute You

47 King Henry's Walk, N1 4NH

Dalston locals are fiercely protective of Tina, We Salute You and the number of coffees chalked up on the clever loyalty wall proves just how much this café is loved. The interior is regularly given over to a local artist to use as an exhibition space and do with whatever they wish; this keeps things interesting and makes for a great talking point. The food is fresh and innovative, and the coffee is among the best in town.

+44(0)20 3119 0047
www.tinawesaluteyou.com
⊖ Dalston Kingsland

MON-FRI. 8:00am – 6:00pm
SAT-SUN. 10:00am – 7:00pm

First opened 2009
Roaster Square Mile Coffee Roasters
Machine La Marzocco Linea, 3 groups
Grinder Anfim

Espresso £2.00
Cappuccino £2.70
Latte £2.70
Flat white £2.70

MAP REF. 92

 COFFEE 4.50 / 5    **OVERALL** 4.25 / 5

Wilton Way Café

63 Wilton Way, E8 1BG

Wilton Way Café combines superb coffee and fresh, simple food with art and music to create an outstanding coffee experience. Incorporating clever modular furniture, rotating art exhibits, a busy coffee bar, a generous display of cakes and treats and a radio corner for live local broadcasts, Wilton's makes excellent use of its intimate but vibrant space. Visit on a sunny Saturday to enjoy a fine cup of coffee on the footpath outside, along with the crowds of faithful Wilton's acolytes.

+44(0)20 7249 0444
www.londonfieldsradio.com
⊖ Hackney Central /
⇌ Hackney Downs Rail

MON-FRI. 8:00am - 5:00pm
SAT. 8:00am - 6:00pm
SUN. 9:00am - 6:00pm

First opened 2009
Roaster Climpson & Sons
Machine La Marzocco Linea, 2 groups
Grinder Mazzer Super Jolly, Anfim

Espresso £1.50 / £1.80
Cappuccino £2.30 / £2.50
Latte £2.30 / £2.50
Flat white £2.30 / £2.50

MAP REF. 93

  COFFEE 4.50 / 5 **OVERALL** 4.50 / 5

THE END OF INSTANT TYRANNY IS HERE.

No longer do the terms 'Pour-over, Chemex, Cafetiere & Aeropress' need to remain terms associated with obscure indie bands from the 90's. No longer do you need to settle for dull, bland, boring same ol', same ol' instant coffee. No longer do you have to be a supercool coffeehouse barista to do it decently either!

Let us show you how to **Make Decent Coffee**, throw away that jar of instant coffee and join the revolution...

Visit **www.makedecentcoffee.com** for all of the tools & knowledge to start making decent coffee at home (or the office) that'll be the envy of all of your friends!

We were voted the
Most Engaging Stand Experience
at The London Coffee Festival 2012.

MAKE DECENT COFFEE

South East

London's thriving South East has welcomed some exciting newcomers on the coffee scene over the past twelve months. It is now also more accessible thanks to the completion of the orbital Overground line from East London to Clapham Junction via Peckham. Along with its vibrant fine food market scene, this area of the city is rapidly establishing itself on the coffee map.

Arlo & Moe

340 Brockley Road, SE4 2BT

NEW

Arlo & Moe is a simply beautiful little neighbourhood café tucked away in Crofton Park. Despite having only opened in September 2012, it has already struck a chord with the locals. Staff and customers mingle freely as cheerful rockabilly tunes fill the air, and children are particularly welcomed. The coffee is locally roasted by Dark Fluid, accompanied by a tempting food menu. Try the signature 'sexy toast' on campaillou bread, or stay awhile and make new friends at one of Arlo & Moe's supper nights.

+44(0)7749 667 207
⇌ Crofton Park Rail

MON-FRI. 7:30am – 4:00pm
SAT-SUN. 10:00am – 4:00pm

First opened 2012
Roaster Dark Fluid
Machine Gaggia, 2 groups
Grinder La Spaziale Astro

Espresso £1.50
Cappuccino £2.30
Latte £2.30 / £3.00
Flat white £2.30

MAP REF.

COFFEE 4.00 / 5

OVERALL 4.00 / 5 ★★★★☆

Browns of Brockley

5 Coulgate Street, SE4 2RW

Browns of Brockley is top dog for coffee in South London. Well-trained staff pull shots on a La Marzocco Strada, and offer single origins on filter. A recent refit preserves the simple layout and natural colour scheme, while making better use of space. Owner Ross Brown is committed to sourcing the highest quality ingredients for both coffee and food. Local suppliers include The Cheeseboard and Drings butchers of Greenwich, whilst Northiam Dairy supplies deliciously sweet milk. The friendly team is completed by Ludd the pug, Browns' lovable canine mascot.

+44(0)20 8692 0722
www.brownsofbrockley.com
⊖ Brockley

MON-FRI. 7:30am - 6:00pm
SAT. 9:00am - 5:00pm
SUN. 10:00am - 4:00pm

First opened 2009
Roaster Square Mile Coffee Roasters
Machine La Marzocco Strada EP, 2 groups
Grinder Mazzer Robur E x2

Espresso £2.00
Cappuccino £3.00
Latte £3.00
Flat white £3.00

MAP REF. **95**

COFFEE
4.75 / 5

OVERALL
4.50 / 5 ★★★★⯪

Café Viva

44 Choumert Road, SE15 4SE

Choumert Road is a true microcosm of South East London. Café Viva squeezes between tranquil Victorian terraces and the colourful mêlée of Rye Lane's African food shops. Volcano Coffee is lovingly served in 70s cups, and tea brewed in owner Lily's collection of Brown Betty teapots. Herself a Goldsmiths College graduate, Lily hosts pieces from local artists, alongside framed messages from Peckham's post-riot 'Peace Wall'. At Café Viva terrific coffee and a strong sense of community go hand in hand.

+44(0)7918 653 533
www.cafeviva.co.uk
⊖ Peckham Rye

MON. Closed
TUE-FRI. 7:30am - 5:00pm
SAT-SUN. 9:00am - 5:00pm

First opened 2012
Roaster Volcano Coffee Works
Machine La Marzocco Linea, 2 groups
Grinder Mazzer Super Jolly

Espresso £1.50 / £1.80
Cappuccino £2.50
Latte £2.50
Flat white £2.50

MAP REF.

 COFFEE 4.00 / 5  OVERALL 4.00 / 5 ★★★★☆

The Deptford Project

121-123 Deptford High Street, SE8 4NS

The Deptford Project is an innovative café in the shell of a decommissioned 1960s train carriage, occupying a site on Deptford High Street since 2008. The Project is a delightfully quirky community hub, particularly on Deptford Market days - Wednesday, Friday and Saturday - when it attracts a constant stream of local artists and residents. Colourful, frequently changing street art covers the exterior of the café, and the outside decking provides the perfect spot to soak up some sunshine on warm days.

+44(0)7545 593 279
www.thedeptfordproject.com
Deptford Bridge DLR / New Cross /
Deptford Rail

MON-SAT. 9:00am - 5:30pm
SUN. 10:00am - 4:30pm

First opened 2010
Roaster Darlington's
Machine La Marzocco Linea, 2 groups
Grinder San Remo

Espresso £1.40
Cappuccino £1.90 / £2.20
Latte £1.90 / £2.20
Flat white £2.10

MAP REF. **97**

COFFEE 3.75 / 5    **OVERALL** 4.00 / 5 ★★★★☆

Fee & Brown

50 High Street, Beckenham, BR3 1AY

 NEW

Fee & Brown has set a new benchmark for coffee in London's suburbs. Husband and wife team Ercan and Del serve a Caravan blend custom-roasted to their specifications. The artisan lunch menu, ample space, and plentiful seating make Fee & Brown an excellent choice for groups. Baked treats fill the counter top, and whole cakes are available to order. A framed notice proclaims the café's dedication to quality coffee, a manifesto resolutely upheld by the team of passionate young baristas.

+44(0)20 8658 1996
Beckenham Junction Rail

MON-FRI. 7:30am - 5:00pm
SAT. 9:00am - 5:00pm
SUN. 10:00am - 4:00pm

First opened 2012
Roaster Caravan bespoke blend
Machine La Marzocco Linea, 3 groups
Grinder Mazzer Robur x3

Espresso £2.20
Cappuccino £2.40
Latte £2.40
Flat white £2.40

MAP REF. **98**

COFFEE 4.25 / 5    **OVERALL** 4.50 / 5 ★★★★⯪

South East

115

Monmouth Coffee Company The Borough

2 Park Street, SE1 9AB

Monmouth Coffee Company has developed a cult-like following among many Londoners who make weekly pilgrimages to this coffee mecca. The Borough Market venue, larger than the Covent Garden premises, is incredibly popular with market regulars and tourists, and is appropriately surrounded by some of the city's finest producers of foods and beverages. Fridays and Saturdays are extremely busy, so a weekday trip is a safer bet. Also worth a visit is Monmouth's new site in Bermondsey, at Arch 3 Spa North, open Saturdays only 8am - 12pm.

+44(0)20 7232 3010
www.monmouthcoffee.co.uk
⊖ London Bridge

Sister locations Covent Garden / Bermondsey

MON-SAT. 7:30am - 6:00pm
SUN. Closed

First opened 2001
Roaster Monmouth Coffee Company
Machine La Marzocco Linea, 2 groups x2
Grinder Mazzer Robur E, Mazzer Robur

Espresso £1.35
Cappuccino £2.35
Latte £2.35
Flat white £2.35

MAP REF.

 COFFEE
4.50 / 5  OVERALL
4.75 / 5 ★ ★ ★ ★ ★

No67 at South London Gallery

67 Peckham Road, SE5 8UH

Set within a handsome townhouse adjoining the South London Gallery, No67 is a popular café and dining room frequently packed out for weekend brunch. At less busy periods it offers a soothing respite from the din of busy Camberwell. With a move to Allpress beans and a machine upgrade, the coffee has improved greatly and is now a strong contender for the area's best cup. Open well into the evening, No67 is also an ideal spot to enjoy cocktails and craft beer with the cultured South London crowd.

+44(0)20 7252 7649
www.number67.co.uk
Peckham Rye / Denmark Hill

MON. Closed
TUE. 8:00am - 6:30pm
WED-FRI. 8:00am - 11:00pm
SAT. 10:00am - 11:00pm
SUN. 10:00am - 6:30pm

First opened 2010
Roaster Allpress Espresso
Machine La Marzocco FB/80, 2 groups
Grinder Mazzer Robur, Mazzer Super Jolly

Espresso £1.30 / £1.80
Cappuccino £2.30 / £2.80
Latte £2.30 / £2.80
Flat white £2.30 / £2.80

MAP REF.

     COFFEE 4.25 / 5

 OVERALL 4.25 / 5

ScooterCaffè

132 Lower Marsh, SE1 7AE

The brainchild of New Zealand ex-aircraft engineer Craig O'Dwyer, ScooterCaffè started life as a Vespa workshop. However, O'Dwyer soon branched out into coffee and now his collection of vintage machinery and scooter memorabilia adorns a truly unique café space. The moody basement area hosts movie, music and comedy nights. Coffee is made on a beautiful 1957 Faema espresso machine, accompanied by vintage grinders. ScooterCaffè is one of London's most unique retro coffee experiences.

+44(0)20 7620 1421
⊖ Lambeth North / Waterloo

Sister locations Cable Café

MON-THU. 8:30am - 11:00pm
FRI. 8:30am - 12:00am
SAT. 10:00am - 12:00am
SUN. 10:00am - 11:00pm

First opened 2009
Roaster Londinium Coffee
Machine 1957 Faema, 3 groups
Grinder Quick Mill, vintage Omer

Espresso £1.50
Cappuccino £2.20
Latte £2.20
Flat white £2.20

MAP REF. 101

 COFFEE 4.00 / 5

OVERALL 4.25 / 5

St. David Coffee House

5 David's Road, SE23 3EP

St. David Coffee House brims with retro charm and has firm roots in the local community. For a short period last year, the café's future became uncertain when the original owners decided to move on, but thankfully new owners Jordan, Russell and Sian have stepped in and continue to serve superb Square Mile coffee to the diverse population of Forest Hill. Local artists, actors, musicians and families come here in droves to sip espresso among the books, stacks of vinyl, and vintage movie memorabilia.

+44(0)20 8291 6646
www.stdavidcoffeehouse.co.uk
⊖ Forest Hill

MON. Closed
TUE-FRI. 8:00am - 6:00pm
SAT. 9:00am - 6:00pm
SUN. 10:00am - 4:00pm

First opened 2010
Roaster Square Mile Coffee Roasters
Machine Rancilio Classe 10
Grinder Anfim

Espresso £1.50 / £1.70
Cappuccino £2.40
Latte £2.40
Flat white £2.30

MAP REF. **102**

COFFEE 4.00 / 5   OVERALL 4.00 / 5 ★★★★☆

Taylor St Baristas Canary Wharf

8 South Colonnade, Canary Wharf, E14 4PZ

This lean, mean café is designed to produce a high volume of quality coffee for the district's bankers and business people. The equipment list includes two 3-group Simonelli Aurelias (for takeaway coffees), one 2-group Synesso (for guest espresso only) and six grinders. Customers can also opt for a single origin AeroPress brew. A full breakfast and brunch menu is on offer, and Australian Freddo chocolate frogs and Caramel Koalas offer a touch of sunshine on a grey London day.

+44(0)20 7519 6536
www.taylor-st.com
⊖ Canary Wharf

Sister locations Richmond / Liverpool Street / Shoreditch / Monument / Bank / Mayfair / South Quay

MON-FRI. 7:00am - 6:00pm
SAT-SUN. Closed

First opened 2011
Roaster Union Hand-Roasted and others
Machine Nuova Simonelli Aurelia x2, Synesso Cyncra
Grinder Mazzer Robur E x2, Mazzer Major E x2, Anfim, Mahlkönig Tanzania

Espresso £1.80
Cappuccino £2.50 / £2.90
Latte £2.50 / £2.90
Flat white £2.50 / £3.40

MAP REF. **103**

COFFEE 4.50 / 5   OVERALL 4.25 / 5 ★★★★☆

Volcano Coffee House

Parkhall Trading Estate, 40 Martell Road, SE21 8EN

Volcano operates from a former electronics factory, surprisingly located among a row of terraced houses. This architecturally impressive building houses the roastery, and a spacious café. Opt for Volcano's own 'Fullsteam' espresso blend, or try a range of single estate filters. A collection of antique coffee machines and a vintage roaster displayed on gallery-style plinths announce the founders' shared love for classic machinery. Volcano resonates with a deep passion for espresso culture, past and present.

+44(0)20 8761 8415
www.volcanocoffeeworks.com
West Norwood Rail / West Dulwich Rail

MON–FRI. 8:00am – 4:00pm
SAT. 10:00am – 4:00pm
SUN. Closed

First opened 2012 (café)
Roaster Volcano Coffee Works
Machine Rocket Linea Professionale, 2 groups
Grinder Mazzer Major, Mazzer Super Jolly

Espresso £1.90
Cappuccino £2.00
Latte £2.00
Flat white £2.00

MAP REF.

COFFEE 4.75 / 5

OVERALL 4.50 / 5 ★★★★⯪

With Jam and Bread

386 Lee High Road, SE12 8RW

Photo courtesy of the venue

With Jam and Bread is a cheerful café in which you could happily spend an entire afternoon. Passionate owner Jennie Milsom is also a food and drink writer. This child-friendly venue combines the best elements of a homely neighbourhood retreat with coffee of a standard rarely encountered in London's suburban belt. Delicious lunch and cake options are also available. Occupying the site of a former art gallery, With Jam and Bread retains an exhibition space towards the rear.

+44(0)20 8318 4040
www.withjamandbread.com
⇌ Lee Rail / Hither Green Rail

MON-FRI. 8:00am - 4:30pm
SAT. 9:30am - 4:00pm
SUN. 9:30am - 3:30pm

First opened 2011
Roaster Dark Fluid
Machine La Marzocco Linea, 2 groups
Grinder Anfim, Gaggia MDF

Espresso £1.80
Cappuccino £2.50
Latte £2.50
Flat white £2.30

MAP REF. 105

COFFEE 4.25 / 5		OVERALL 4.25 / 5	

South West

South West London contains a dizzying array of cultural influences, from the Afro-Caribbean heritage of Brixton to the antipodean-influenced lifestyle of Clapham and the genteel suburban rhythms of Putney. The area's colourful and creative coffee culture reflects these unique influences and local quirks.

Artisan Putney

203 Upper Richmond Road, Putney, SW15 6SG

Artisan's motto is "Obsessively passionate about coffee", which is an apt philosophy for this charming Putney café. Artisan's warm, light-filled space is imbued with the aroma of freshly ground Allpress coffee and furnished with quirky designer furniture. Fine artisan foods from local suppliers are displayed on the corrugated iron counter and local mums take advantage of the friendly welcome and pram space. Artisan's inventive loyalty scheme allows customers to spin a wheel to determine their reward.

+44(0)20 8617 3477
www.artisancoffee.co.uk
East Putney / Putney Rail

Sister locations Stamford Brook

MON-FRI. 7:00am - 6:00pm
SAT. 8:00am - 6:00pm
SUN. 8:30am - 6:00pm

First opened 2011
Roaster Allpress Espresso
Machine La Marzocco FB/80
Grinder Mazzer Robur, Mazzer Super Jolly

Espresso £1.50 / £1.90
Cappuccino £2.20 / £2.50
Latte £2.20 / £2.50
Flat white £2.20 / £2.50

MAP REF.

COFFEE 4.50 / 5  OVERALL 4.50 / 5

Birdhouse

123 St John's Hill, SW11 1SZ

This perfectly formed café is a striking addition to St John's Hill in Clapham. Coffee is carefully prepared and served in an interior that is light, beautifully furnished in brushed steel, grey felt and vintage wood, and punctuated with splashes of bright yellow. Bird images adorn the walls, and yellow mesh baskets complete the avian feel. Fresh sandwiches, cookies and cakes are arrayed on an old carpenter's block. Fresh baked eggs are a speciality served only on Fridays and at weekends.

+44(0)20 7228 6663
www.birdhou.se
⊖ Clapham Junction

MON-FRI. 7:00am - 4:00pm
SAT-SUN. 9:00am - 5:00pm

First opened 2011
Roaster Climpson & Sons
Machine La Marzocco Linea, 3 groups
Grinder Anfim

Espresso £2.00
Cappuccino £2.40
Latte £2.40
Flat white £2.40

MAP REF.

COFFEE 4.50 / 5	🫘🫘🫘🫘🫘	OVERALL 4.25 / 5	★★★★✦

The Black Lab Coffee House

18 Clapham Common Southside, SW4 7AB

The Black Lab Coffee House is a warm and cosy choice in an area surprisingly light on good cafés. This venue combines Italian influences with a London roast by Climpson & Sons to create coffee that is rooted in the past but in touch with modern tastes. The Black Lab serves a range of pastries and cakes sourced from a local patisserie. It's a great spot to spend a Sunday morning reading the papers over a cappuccino, or to grab a takeaway coffee on the way to nearby Clapham Common.

+44(0)20 7738 8441
www.blacklabcoffee.com
⊖ Clapham Common

MON-FRI. 7:30am – 5:30pm
SAT-SUN. 9:00am – 5:00pm

First opened 2010
Roaster Climpson & Sons
Machine Gaggia D90, 2 groups
Grinder Mahlkönig K30, Mazzer Super Jolly

Espresso £1.80
Cappuccino £2.40
Latte £2.50
Flat white £2.40

MAP REF.

    COFFEE 4.00 / 5   OVERALL 4.00 / 5 ★★★★☆

Brew Clapham

45 Northcote Road, SW11 1NJ

A favourite with the Northcote Road set, Brew is a cheerful antidote to the many chain coffee stores nearby. Simple and cosy, Brew offers Union coffee and a comprehensive menu in a breezy, laidback environment. However, this café is best known for its sensational breakfasts, which feature only the best-quality local ingredients, as well as juices and smoothies. A tantalising dinner menu is also on offer and is complemented by a beer and wine list.

+44(0)20 7585 2198
www.brew-cafe.com
⊖ Clapham Junction

Sister locations Wimbledon

MON-SAT. 7:00am - 10:00pm
SUN. 7:00am - 6:00pm

First opened 2008
Roaster Union Hand-Roasted
Machine La Marzocco Linea, 2 groups
Grinder Mazzer

Espresso £2.00 / £2.20
Cappuccino £2.80
Latte £2.80
Flat white £2.80

MAP REF.

Federation Coffee

Unit 77-78 Brixton Village Market, Coldharbour Lane, SW9 8PS

Since opening in the redeveloped Brixton Village Market in 2010, Federation has led a flowering of foodie culture in Brixton. Having moved to a larger site within the market due to its popularity, it is now surrounded by a host of other cafés following its lead. Federation now has an off-site roasting operation, and has upped the ante in the café with the installation of a high-end Synesso machine. Head barista, Edita, is an expert hand, and recently competed in the Lithuanian Barista Championship.

www.federationcoffee.com
 Brixton

Sister locations Brighton Terrace kiosk

MON–FRI. 8:00am - 5:00pm
SAT. 9:00am - 6:00pm
SUN. 9:00am - 5:00pm

First opened 2010
Roaster Federation
Machine Synesso Cyncra, 3 groups
Grinder Mazzer Robur

Espresso £1.90
Cappuccino £2.50
Latte £2.50
Flat white £2.50

MAP REF. 110

 COFFEE 4.50 / 5   OVERALL 4.50 / 5

Grind Coffee Bar Putney

79 Lower Richmond Road, SW15 1ET

This stylish, contemporary café was one of the pioneers on the now-thriving Putney coffee scene. Grind's friendly antipodean atmosphere and excellent flat whites make it popular with local ex-pats, but its bespoke house blend from London Coffee Roasters and use of British ingredients give it a decidedly local outlook. The café's corner location and tempting range of homemade cakes and savouries make it difficult to pass without popping in for a coffee and a chat with the genial team of baristas.

+44(0)20 8789 5101
www.grindcoffeebar.co.uk
⊖ Putney Bridge

Sister locations Westfield Stratford / Battersea

MON-FRI. 7:00am - 5:00pm
SAT-SUN. 8:30am - 5:00pm

First opened 2010
Roaster London Coffee Roasters
Machine La Marzocco Strada EP, 2 groups
Grinder Mazzer Robur x2

Espresso £1.80
Cappuccino £2.30 / £2.70
Latte £2.30 / £2.70
Flat white £2.30 / £2.70

MAP REF. 111

 COFFEE 4.50 / 5

 OVERALL 4.25 / 5 ★★★★✬

129

M1lk

20 Bedford Hill, SW12 9RG

 NEW

Photo courtesy of the venue

M1lk is a magnificent medley of artisan coffee and Aussie-style food, with a sprinkling of British eccentricity. The playful and nostalgic theme borders on the bizarre with the café's baby head motif. The hip team take their espresso very seriously, squeezing every drop of performance from their modified Linea. Alternatively, try an AeroPress to appreciate the subtleties of the single origins on offer. Cupping classes are also available for those interested in developing their own coffee expertise.

+44(0)20 8772 9085
www.m1lk.co.uk
⊖ Balham

MON-SAT. 8:00am - 5:00pm
SUN. 9:00am - 5:00pm

First opened 2012
Roaster Workshop Coffee Co.
Machine La Marzocco Linea PID, 2 groups
Grinder Anfim, Mazzer Robur E

Espresso £2.00
Cappuccino £2.20
Latte £2.30
Flat white £2.20

MAP REF. **112**

 COFFEE 4.50 / 5  **OVERALL** 4.25 / 5 ★★★★☆

The Roastery

789 Wandsworth Rd, SW8 3JQ

The Roastery is an unassuming café that lays claim to being the first antipodean coffee roaster in London. The venue roasts using an old Turkish Toper machine, and markets its beans under the Bullet Coffee label. The best time to visit The Roastery is at a weekend, when enthusiastic Wandsworth regulars come out in force to feast on the hearty brunch offerings. The scrumptious antipodean-inspired menu includes French toast and corn fritters with asparagus and bacon.

+44(0)20 7350 1961
www.bullet-coffee.com
⊖ Clapham Common

MON-FRI. 7:30am - 3:30pm
SAT-SUN. 9:00am - 3:30pm

First opened 2009
Roaster Bullet Coffee Cartel
Machine La Marzocco Linea PID, 3 groups
Grinder Mazzer Super Jolly

Espresso £1.50
Cappuccino £2.40
Latte £2.40
Flat white £2.40

MAP REF. **113**

COFFEE 4.25 / 5		OVERALL 4.00 / 5	★★★★☆

Tried & True

279 Upper Richmond Road, SW15 6SP

Tried & True brings the best of Kiwi café culture to suburban Putney. The vibe is relaxed and welcoming. The interior eschews voguish shabby chic in favour of a bright, clean and refreshingly modern aesthetic. The baristas pull shots with utmost care, constantly re-calibrating the equipment to keep the Square Mile coffee spot on. A beautiful garden beckons in the summer months, and the delectable brunch menu has few rivals. Tried & True is one of a rare breed of top-class neighbourhood cafés.

+44(0)20 8789 0410
www.triedandtruecafe.co.uk
⊖ Putney

MON-FRI. 7:30am - 4:00pm
SAT-SUN. 8:30am - 4:30pm

First opened 2012
Roaster Square Mile Coffee Roasters
Machine La Marzocco FB/80, 3 groups
Grinder Mazzer Robur E, Mazzer Super Jolly

Espresso £1.50 / £2.00
Cappuccino £2.20 / £2.50
Latte £2.20 / £2.50
Flat white £2.50

MAP REF. **114**

COFFEE 4.50 / 5		OVERALL 4.25 / 5	★★★★☆

Coffee looks better...
...*well dressed*

HUHTAMAKI

To find out more about our comprehensive range of cups and lids call Huhtamaki on **02392 512434**
www.foodservice.huhtamaki.co.uk

West

Home to some of London's wealthiest residents, world-renowned museums and lavish department stores, West London has a well established café culture. The number of quality-focussed coffee bars has grown in recent months, but still has a long way to go to match other London neighbourhoods.

Artisan Stamford Brook

372 King Street, W6 0RX

Photo courtesy of the venue

Owners Edwin and Magda's passion for coffee began with a trip to Uganda, where they contributed to development work with coffee farmers. Back home in London, they lead a team of baristas who are resolutely committed to getting the very best from their coffee. Artisan's second venue in Stamford Brook upholds the high standards of coffee excellence the company has become known for. Electric blue walls contrast with the copper counter and stools, creating a very striking piece of café design.

+44(0)20 3302 1434
www.artisancoffee.co.uk
Stamford Brook

Sister locations Putney

MON-FRI. 7:30am - 5:30pm
SAT-SUN. 8:30am - 5:30pm

First opened 2013
Roaster Allpress Espresso
Machine La Marzocco FB/80, 3 groups
Grinder Mazzer Robur, Mazzer Super Jolly

Espresso £1.50 / £1.90
Cappuccino £2.20 / £2.50
Latte £2.20 / £2.50
Flat white £2.20 / £2.50

MAP REF. 115

COFFEE 4.50 / 5

OVERALL 4.50 / 5 ★★★★✦

Barossa

277 New Kings Road, SW6 4RD

Barossa, formerly known as Di'Zain, is a stylish café in an area otherwise lacking quality coffee shops. Barossa's interior is modern and sophisticated, the baristas are friendly and the brunch menu offers something to suit all tastes. Caravan coffee is expertly prepared on a La Marzocco Linea, a true workhorse for London's artisan coffee purveyors. Barossa is an Aussie favourite which has become a neighbourhood gem for Fulham locals.

+44(0)20 7751 9711
Parsons Green

MON-FRI. 8:00am – 5:00pm
SAT. 9:00am – 5:00pm
SUN. 9:00am – 4:00pm

First opened 2009
Roaster Caravan
Machine La Marzocco Linea, 2 groups
Grinder Mazzer Robur E

Espresso £1.80
Cappuccino £2.50
Latte £2.60
Flat white £2.50

MAP REF. 116

  COFFEE 4.00 / 5   **OVERALL** 4.00 / 5

Electric Coffee Co.

40 Haven Green, Ealing, W5 2NX

Stepping inside this Ealing enclave, one's gaze is immediately stolen by the Kees Van Der Westen Mirage coffee machine. Crafted with aircraft-grade aluminium, this stunning machine is the supercharged dynamo of Electric Coffee Co. Piloted by an enthusiastic team, the Mirage fires out gutsy espresso custom roasted by Volcano Coffee Works. Filter coffee is also available should you prefer a more gentle take-off. Electric is unequivocally the highest flying third wave coffee shop in the west.

+44(0)20 8997 8338
www.electriccoffee.co.uk
⊖ Ealing Broadway

MON-FRI. 7:00am – 6:00pm
SAT. 8:00am – 6:00pm
SUN. 9:00am – 5:00pm

First opened 2008
Roaster Volcano Coffee Works bespoke blend
Machine Kees Van Der Westen Mirage Veloce, 3 groups
Grinder Mazzer Robur E, Anfim Super Caimano

Espresso £1.90
Cappuccino £2.40 / £2.60
Latte £2.40 / £2.60
Flat white £2.40

MAP REF.

COFFEE 4.50 / 5

OVERALL 4.25 / 5 ★★★★

Fernandez & Wells South Kensington

43 Lexington Street, W1F 9AL

Fernandez & Wells' most recent venue is a godsend for coffee-starved West Londoners and visitors to the nearby museums. The interior's high ceiling and elegant cornicing resonate with South Kensington's noble architecture. Cured meats hang artfully against the rear wall, accompanied by a shelf of well-chosen wines. There's plenty of seating round the back, which is fortunate as you'll almost certainly want to complement your Has Bean coffee with a dish from the fine deli menu.

+44(0)20 7589 7473
www.fernandezandwells.com
⊖ South Kensington

Sister locations Somerset House / St Anne's Court / Beak Street / Lexington Street

MON-FRI. 8:00am - 10:00pm
SAT-SUN. 9:00am - 10:00pm

First opened 2012
Roaster Has Bean bespoke blend
Machine Synesso Cyncra, 3 groups
Grinder Mazzer Robur E x2, Mahlkönig Tanzania

Espresso £2.30
Cappuccino £2.60
Latte £2.60
Flat white £2.60

MAP REF. 118

COFFEE 4.50 / 5		OVERALL 4.25 / 5	★★★★✦

Loft Coffee Company

4 Canfield Gardens, NW6 3BS

What Loft lacks in space, it compensates for with exceptionally friendly service, a welcome remedy to the scrum of Finchley Road. Sung-Jae Lee and his wife have created an uncomplicated, whitewashed space with warm wood panelling and a small number of tables. Since opening late last year, locals in the know have largely had Loft all to themselves. Grinding excellent Monmouth beans in an area not known for artisan coffee, Loft is a blessing for North West Londoners in search of a quality cup.

⊖ Finchley Road

MON-FRI. 7:00am - 5:00pm
SAT. 8:00am - 4:00pm
SUN. 10:00am - 1:00pm

First opened 2012
Roaster Monmouth Coffee Company
Machine La Marzocco Linea, 3 groups
Grinder Mazzer Super Jolly

Espresso £2.10
Cappuccino £2.60
Latte £2.60
Flat white £2.60

MAP REF. 119

COFFEE 4.00 / 5		OVERALL 4.00 / 5	★★★★☆

TomTom Coffee House

114 Ebury Street, SW1W 9QD

Set in leafy Belgravia, Tomtom Coffee House is a neighbourhood favourite with an upmarket feel. A large round table and abundance of natural light fosters a friendly and communal atmosphere, making this a lovely choice for a lazy afternoon coffee hangout with friends. Tomtom roasts its own coffee as well as several other house blends that are available for customers to purchase. Sister shop Tomtom Cigars is conveniently located across the road on Elizabeth Street.

+44(0)20 7730 1771
www.tomtom.co.uk
⊖ Victoria / Sloane Square

MON-FRI. 8:00am - 5:00pm
SAT. 9:00am - 6:00pm
SUN. 9:00am - 5:00pm

First opened 2008
Roaster Tomtom
Machine La Marzocco Linea, 2 groups
Grinder Mazzer, Mahlkönig Guatemala

Espresso £1.80
Cappuccino £2.60
Latte £2.60
Flat white £2.90

MAP REF.

 COFFEE 4.00 / 5 **OVERALL** 4.00 / 5 ★★★★☆

Coffee Knowledge

Behind every cup of coffee is a unique story. On its journey from coffee tree to cup, coffee passes through the hands of a number of skilled individuals. Over the following pages, expert contributors share their specialist knowledge. As you will see, the coffee we enjoy is the result of a rich and complex process, and there is always something new to learn.

Coffee at Origin

by **Mike Riley**, Falcon Speciality Green Coffee Importers

If you go into London's vibrant coffee community today and ask any good barista what makes a perfect cup of coffee, they will always tell you that it starts with the bean. Beyond the roasting technique, the perfect grind, and exact temperatures and precision pressure of a modern espresso machine, we must look to the dedicated coffee farmer who toils away in the tropical lands of Africa, Asia and Latin America. They are the first heroes of our trade.

Approximately 25 million people in over 50 countries are involved in producing coffee. The bean, or seed to be exact, is extracted from cherries that most commonly ripen red but sometimes orange or yellow. The cherries are usually hand-picked then processed by various means. Sometimes they are dried in the fruit under tropical sunshine until they resemble raisins – a process known as 'natural'. The 'honey process' involves pulping the fresh cherries to extract the beans which are then sundried, still coated in their sticky mucilage. Alternatively, in the 'washed process', the freshly pulped beans are left to stand in tanks of water for several hours where enzyme activity breaks down the mucilage, before they are sundried on concrete patios or raised beds. Each method has a profound impact on the ultimate flavour of the coffee.

The term 'speciality coffee' is used to differentiate the world's best from the rest. This means it has to be Arabica, the species of coffee that is often bestowed with incredible flavours - unlike its hardy cousin Robusta which is usually reserved for commercial products and many instant blends. But being Arabica alone is by no means enough for a coffee to achieve the speciality tag, since the best beans are usually those grown at higher altitude on rich and fertile soils. As well as country and region of origin, the variety is important too; Bourbon, Typica, Caturra, Catuai, Pacamara and Geisha to name but a few. Just as Shiraz and Chardonnay grapes have their own complex flavours, the same is true of coffee's varieties. Some of the world's most amazing coffees are the result of the farmer's innovative approach to experimentation with growing and production techniques, meaning that today's speciality roaster is able to source coffees of incredible complexity and variation.

A good coffee establishment will showcase coffees when they are at their best – freshly harvested and seasonal, just like good fruit and vegetables. Seasonal espresso blends change throughout the year to reflect this.

As speciality coffee importers we source stand-out coffees by regularly travelling to origin countries. Direct trade with farmers is always our aim. Above all, we pay sustainable prices and encourage them to treat their land, and those who work it, with respect. Such an approach is increasingly demanded by London's speciality coffee community in order to safeguard the industry's future.

Small Batch Roasting

by **Kurt Stewart**, Roaster and Co-owner, Volcano Coffee Works

I was brought up in a household dedicated to pickling, baking, sauce making and preserving. After experimenting with home brewing and wine making, my first foray into the aromatic world of small batch roasting was inevitable.

My own first experiments in small batch roasting started at home with some green beans and a wok. Of course roasting at home is much like home cooking, but when the term is applied to a commercial enterprise, it encompasses the passion and adventure of a home cook with the control and precision of a gourmet chef.

The art behind developing and building a roasting profile for a particular coffee is approached in the same way a chef develops cuisine, or a vintner crafts a wine. Culinary rules and science apply in equal measure. The roaster builds layers of flavour, working with the ingredients, sometimes pushing or manipulating the properties of an individual bean, to achieve the desired balance of sweetness, acidity, body, and the right mouth-feel and aftertaste. Coffee and wine share a vocabulary of descriptors, but as coffee has more flavour molecules than wine, coffee descriptors reach further into the culinary world. You will hear words describing aspects of flavour and taste senses, such as fruit acidity, sweet roundness, viscous syrup body, juicy plum, creamy, buttery, velvet chocolate textures. Delicious!

When a green bean is roasted, three fundamental processes occur that impact the flavours of the bean: enzyme by-products develop (giving the floral, citrus and fruity aromas), sugars brown (giving the sweet, caramel and nutty aromas), and plant fibres in the bean are roasted, known as dry-distillation (giving the spicy and smokey flavours). Only the enzyme by-products (which come from the coffee plant itself) are due to the bean chosen for roasting, whilst the remaining two processes are the result of how the bean is roasted. This is why no two small batch roasters will create an identical flavour profile from the same bean. Like chefs, each roaster will identify with, single out and highlight a flavour or combination of flavours which pleases, satisfies or amazes their palate.

Small Batch Roasting is a term reserved for those using roasting equipment controlled by the human hand rather than computers. A skilled roaster who understands his equipment, maintains ducting, understands heat/air ratios and extraction principles, coupled with following some basic fundamentals, can draw out origin characteristics and individual nuances, and create a roast where the optimum flavour potential is realised.

The roasting equipment itself is fundamentally a steel drum, which is usually heated by a gas flame. The drum constantly revolves, and at around 10 minutes of roasting at 203-205°C the developing beans reach 'first crack' (a bit like popcorn cracking). If roasting stops here, it will be a mild or lighter roast. When roasting continues, samples are taken with every revolution of the drum and the roaster observes the developing bean's colour, mass and aroma. The roaster may apply more or less heat or air and will remove the beans once they have reached the desired roast profile. This is usually within a 20 minute roasting time and often before second crack is reached as beyond this point the beans can lose their subtle origin characteristics and begin to take on a generic burnt flavour. The beans then enter the cooling tray until cool to touch. This process is in stark contrast to the large scale computer controlled commercial roasting process that takes between 90 seconds and 10 minutes at temperatures in excess of 360°C. The beans are then doused with water to cool them. Although this is the most economic way to roast beans, it takes away any input by the roaster and does not give the bean enough time to develop fully.

When a roastery operation gets to such a scale that the roaster becomes distanced from their beans due to mechanised roasting processes and machinery, the instinct and hands-on effect that define a small batch roaster's product will always become somewhat diminished. And therein lies the excitement and diversity that small batch roasting offers over and above large-scale operations. It comes down to the physical ability of a talented roaster to exercise his or her senses, passion, enthusiasm, and the art of roasting.

Coffee Tasting

by **Lynsey Harley**, National Coordinator UK Chapter, Speciality Coffee Association of Europe,

Coffee tasting is the process of identifying the characteristics of a particular coffee. In the coffee industry, professional 'cupping' sessions are conducted to evaluate coffees on a range of attributes. Cupping helps coffee buyers select which coffees to buy, and identify desirable attributes for formulating blends.

Coffee is most commonly scored using The Specialty Coffee Association of America (SCAA) system. Coffees achieving a score of 85 or higher (from a maximum of 100) are regarded as 'specialty' grade. These coffees have no defects and have a very distinct pleasant flavour profile. Coffees are scored on the following attributes: aroma, flavour, aftertaste, acidity, body, sweetness, cleanliness, uniformity and balance.

The cupping process follows a set procedure: 8.25g of coarsely ground coffee is measured into a shallow cup, specifically designed for the purpose. 150ml of water heated to 92°C is added and left for 4 minutes. Next, a spoon is used to break and remove the 'crust', which provides the first opportunity to sample the coffee's aroma. After a further 6 minutes, the cupper begins to taste the coffee. Different attributes are evaluated at intervals as the coffee cools.

70°C: Flavour and Aftertaste

Flavour: The coffee's principle flavour; what are your taste buds telling you?

Aftertaste: The length of positive flavour qualities after the coffee has been swallowed.

70°C – 60°C: Acidity and Body

Acidity: Bright for positive acidity, sour for negative. Positive acidity adds to the coffee's sweetness.

Body: The 'weight' of the brew. Is it heavy like a good red wine, or light and refined like a sauvignon blanc?

38°C: Sweetness and Cleanliness.

Sweetness: Is the coffee sweet and pleasing?

Cleanliness: When no defects are found, the cup is clean.

Balance: Greater than the sum of its parts. Flavour, aftertaste, acidity and body work together to achieve balance.

One coffee can taste dramatically different depending on the processing method. Washing coffees increases the acidity, whilst the semi-washed process gives a honeyed sweetness to the coffee. The natural processing method can increase the sweetness, and can also encourage development of more obscure flavours including strawberry, blueberry and creamy notes.

Tasting coffee at home can be fun; exploring what a coffee can offer in terms of flavour, sweetness and other attributes is exciting. Your local speciality coffee shop can offer advice on which coffees are in season, and many will sell beans for you to experiment with at home. There's a coffee out there for everyone.

SCAA Coffee taster's wheel

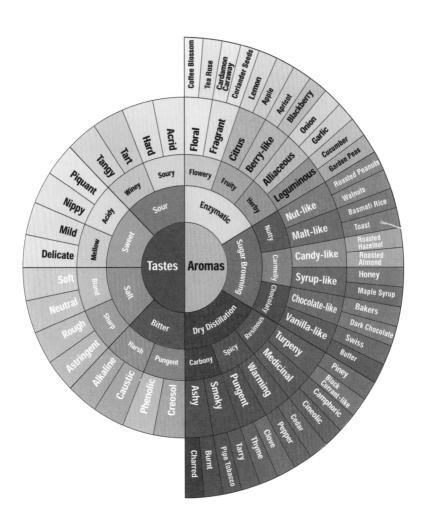

Brewing Filter Coffee at Home

by **Christian Baker, David Robson & Sam Mason**, Association Coffee

Y ou may be surprised to know that filter coffee brewed at home can rival that of your favourite coffee shop. All you need is good quality ingredients and some inexpensive equipment. Keep in mind that small variations in grind coarseness, coffee / water ratio and brew time will make a significant difference to flavour, and that trial and error is the key to unlocking perfection.

Whole Beans: Whole bean coffee is superior to pre-ground. Coffee rapidly deteriorates once ground, so buy your coffee in whole bean form and store it in an air-tight container at room temperature. It should be consumed between three and thirty days after roast and ground only moments before brewing.

Water: Water is important because it makes up over 98% of the finished drink. Only use bottled water, preferably with a dry residue between 80-150mg/l. London tap water is not suitable for brewing - it will inhibit your ability to extract flavour and reveal only a fraction of a coffee's potential.

Digital scales: Get a set of scales accurate to 1g and large enough to hold your coffee brewer. Coffee is commonly measured in 'scoops' or 'tablespoons', but coffee and water are best measured by weight for greater accuracy and to ensure repeatability. Small changes in the ratio of coffee to water can have a significant impact on flavour. A good starting point is 60-70g of coffee per litre of water. Apply this ratio to meet the size of your brewer.

Grinder

A burr grinder is essential. Burr grinders are superior to blade grinders because they allow the grind coarseness to be set and produce a more consistent size of coffee fragment (critical for an even extraction). As a general rule, the coarser the grind the longer the brew time required, and vice versa. For example, an espresso needs a very fine grind whereas a French Press works with a coarser grind.

French Press

Preheat the French Press with hot water, and discard. Add 34g of coarsely ground coffee and pour in 500g of water just below boiling point (94/95˚C). Steep for 4 to 5 minutes then gently plunge to the bottom. Decant the coffee straight away to avoid over-brewing (known as over-extraction).

AeroPress

The AeroPress is wonderfully versatile. It can be used with finely ground coffee and a short steep time, or with a coarser grind and a longer steep time. The latter is our preferred method for its flavour and repeatability. Preheat the AeroPress using hot water, and discard. Rinse the paper filter before securing, and place the AeroPress over a sturdy cup or jug. Add 16g of coffee and pour in 240g of water at 95˚C. Secure the plunger on top, creating a seal. Steep for 3 minutes then plunge over 20 seconds.

Pour Over

We recommend using a pouring kettle for better pouring control. Place a filter paper in the cone and rinse through with hot water. Add 15g of coffee and slowly pour 30g of 95°C water to pre-soak the coffee grounds. This creates the 'bloom'. After 30 seconds add 250g of water, pouring steadily in a circular motion over the centre. It should take 1 minute and 45 seconds to pour and between 30-45 seconds to drain through. The key is to keep the flow of water steady. If the water drains too quickly/slowly, adjust the coarseness of the grind to compensate.

Stovetop

A stovetop will not make an espresso, it will, however, make a strong coffee. Pour hot water in to the base to the fill-line or just below the pressure release valve. Fill the basket with ground coffee of medium coarseness (between Pour Over and French Press). Traditional wisdom suggests a fine grind in pursuit of espresso, but stovetops extract differently to espresso machines and grinding fine is a recipe for bitter, over-extracted coffee. Screw the base to the top and place on the heat. When you hear bubbling, remove immediately and decant to ensure the brewing has stopped.

Illustrations: Zoë Barker

The**Coffee**
ArtProject

Share your passion for coffee and art

Submissions invited

www.coffeeartproject.com

@TheCoffeeArtPro

Coffee Glossary

Acidity: the pleasant tartness of a coffee. Examples of acidity descriptors include lively and flat. One of the principal attributes evaluated by professional tasters when determining the quality of a coffee.

AeroPress: a hand-powered coffee brewer marketed by Aerobie Inc., and launched in 2005. Consists of two cylinders, one sliding within the other, somewhat resembling a large syringe. Water is forced through ground coffee held in place by a paper filter, creating a concentrated filter brew.

Affogato: one or more scoops of vanilla ice cream topped with a shot of espresso, served as a dessert.

Americano, Caffè Americano: a long coffee consisting of espresso with hot water added on top. Originates from the style of coffee favoured by American GIs stationed in Europe during WWII.

Arabica, Coffea arabica: the earliest cultivated species of coffee tree and the most widely grown, Arabica accounts for approximately 70% of the world's coffee. Superior in quality to Robusta, it is more delicate and is generally grown at higher altitudes.

Aroma: the fragrance produced by brewed coffee. Examples of aroma descriptors include earthy, spicy and floral. One of the principal attributes evaluated by professional tasters when determining the quality of a coffee.

Barista: a professional person skilled in making coffee, particularly one working at an espresso bar.

Blend: a combination of coffees from different countries or regions. Mixed together, they achieve a balanced flavour profile no single coffee can offer alone.

Body: describes the heaviness, thickness or relative weight of coffee on the tongue. One of the principal attributes evaluated by professional tasters when determining the quality of a coffee.

Bottomless portafilter, naked portafilter: a portafilter without spouts, allowing espresso to flow directly from the bottom of the filter basket into the cup. Allows the extraction to be monitored visually.

Brew group: the assembly protruding from the front of an espresso machine consisting of the grouphead, portafilter and basket. The brew group must be heated to a sufficient temperature to produce a good espresso.

Brew pressure: pressure of 9 bar is required for espresso extraction.

Brew temperature: the water temperature at the point of contact with coffee. Optimum brew temperature varies by extraction method. Espresso brew temperature is typically 90-95°C. A stable brew temperature is crucial for good espresso.

Brew time, extraction time: the contact time between water and coffee. Espresso brew time is typically 25-30 seconds. Brew times are dictated by a variety of factors including the grind coarseness and degree of roast.

Burr set: an integral part of a coffee

grinder. Consists of a pair of rotating steel discs between which coffee beans are ground. Burrs are either flat or conical in shape.

Café con leche: a traditional Spanish coffee consisting of espresso topped with scalded milk.

Café mocha, mocha: similar to a caffè latte, but with added chocolate syrup or powder.

Caffeine: an odourless, slightly bitter alkaloid responsible for the stimulating effect of coffee.

Cappuccino: a classic Italian coffee comprising one-third espresso, one-third steamed milk and one-third frothed milk. Traditionally 4.5oz, but in the UK usually larger. Sometimes topped with powdered chocolate or cinnamon.

Cherry: the fruit of the coffee plant. Each cherry contains two coffee seeds (beans).

Cortado: a traditional short Spanish coffee consisting of espresso cut with a small quantity of steamed milk. Similar to an Italian piccolo.

Crema: the dense caramel-coloured layer that forms on the surface of an espresso. Consists of emulsified oils created by the dispersion of gases in liquid at high pressure. The presence of crema is commonly equated with a good espresso.

Cupping: a method by which professional tasters perform sensory evaluation of coffee. Hot water is poured over ground coffee and left to extract. The taster first samples the aroma, then tastes the coffee by slurping it from a spoon.

Dispersion screen, shower screen: a component of the grouphead that ensures even distribution of brewing water over the coffee bed in the filter basket.

Dosage: the mass of ground coffee used for a given brewing method. Espresso dosage is typically 7-10g of ground coffee (14-20g for a double).

Double espresso, doppio: typically 30-50ml extracted from 14-20g of ground coffee. Most coffee beverages are based on double espresso rather than single.

Drip method: a brewing method that allows brew water to seep through a bed of ground coffee by gravity, not pressure.

Espresso: the short, strong shot of coffee that forms the basis for many other coffee beverages. Made by forcing hot water at high pressure through a compressed bed of finely ground coffee.

Espresso machine: in a typical configuration, a pump delivers hot water from a boiler to the brew group, where it is forced under pressure through ground coffee held in the portafilter. A separate boiler delivers steam for milk foaming.

Extraction: the process of infusing coffee with hot water to release flavour, accomplished either by allowing ground coffee to sit in hot water for a period of time or by forcing hot water through ground coffee under pressure.

Filter method: any brewing method in which water filters through a bed of ground coffee. Most commonly used to describe drip method brewers that use a paper filter to separate grounds from brewed coffee.

Flat white: an espresso-based beverage first made popular in Australia and New Zealand. Made with a double shot of espresso with finely steamed milk and a thin layer of microfoam. Typically served as a 5-6oz drink with latte art.

Flavour: the way a coffee tastes. Flavour descriptors include nutty and earthy. One of the principal attributes evaluated by professional tasters when determining the quality of a coffee.

French press, plunger pot, cafetiere: a brewing method that separates grounds from brewed coffee by pressing them to the bottom of the brewing receptacle with a mesh filter attached to a plunger.

Froth, foam: created when milk is heated and aerated, usually with hot steam from an espresso machine's steam wand. Used to create a traditional cappuccino.

Green coffee, green beans: unroasted coffee. The dried seeds from the coffee cherry.

Grind: the degree of coarseness to which coffee beans are ground. A crucial factor in determining the nature of a coffee brew. Grind coarseness should be varied in accordance with the brewing method. Methods involving longer brew times call for a coarse grind. A fine grind is required for brew methods with a short extraction time such as espresso.

Grinder: a vital piece of equipment for making coffee. Coffee beans must be ground evenly for a good extraction. Most commonly motorised, but occasionally manual. Burr grinders are the best choice for an even grind.

Group: see Brew Group

Grouphead: a component of the brew group containing the locking connector for the portafilter and the dispersion screen.

Latte, caffè latte: an Italian beverage made with espresso combined with steamed milk, traditionally topped with foamed milk and served in a glass. Typically at least 8oz in volume, usually larger.

Latte art: the pattern or design created by pouring steamed milk on top of espresso. Only finely steamed milk is suitable for creating latte art. Popular patterns include the rosetta and heart.

Lever espresso machine: lever machines use manual force to drive a piston that generates the pressure required for espresso extraction. Common in the first half of the 20th century, but now largely superseded by electric pump-driven machines. Lever machines retain a small but passionate group of proponents.

Long black: a coffee beverage made by adding an espresso on top of hot water. Similar to an Americano, but usually shorter and the crema is preserved.

Macchiato: a coffee beverage consisting of espresso 'stained' with a dash of steamed milk (espresso macchiato) or a tall glass of steamed milk 'stained' with espresso (latte macchiato).

Macrofoam: stiff foam containing large bubbles used to make a traditional cappuccino. Achieved by incorporating a greater quantity of air during the milk steaming process.

Microfoam: the preferred texture of finely-steamed milk for espresso-based coffee drinks. Essential for pouring latte art. Achieved by incorporating a lesser quantity of air during the milk steaming process.

Micro-lot coffee: coffee originating from a small, discrete area within a farm, typically benefiting from conditions favourable to the development of a particular set of characteristics. Micro-lot coffees tend to fetch higher prices due to their unique nature.

Over extracted: describes coffee with a bitter or burnt taste, resulting from ground coffee exposed to hot water for too long.

Piccolo: a short Italian coffee beverage made with espresso topped with an equal quantity of steamed milk. Traditionally served in a glass.

Pod: a self-contained, pre-ground, pre-pressed puck of coffee, individually wrapped inside a perforated paper filter. Mostly found in domestic espresso machines. Often compatible only with certain equipment brands.

Pour over: a type of drip filter method in which a thin, steady stream of water is poured slowly over a bed of ground coffee contained within a filter cone.

Pouring kettle: a kettle with a curved, narrow spout specifically designed to deliver a steady, thin stream of water.

Portafilter: consists of a handle (usually plastic) attached to a metal cradle that holds the filter basket. Inserted into the group head and locked in place in preparation for making an espresso. Usually features a single or double spout on the underside to direct the flow of coffee into a cup.

Portafilter basket: a flat bottomed, bowl-shaped metal insert that sits in the portafilter and holds a bed of ground coffee. The basket has an array of tiny holes in the base allowing extracted coffee to seep through and pour into a cup.

Puck: immediately after an espresso extraction, the bed of spent coffee grounds forms compressed waste matter resembling a small hockey puck.

Pull: the act of pouring an espresso. The term originates from the first half of the 20th century when manual machines were the norm, and baristas pulled a lever to create an espresso.

Ristretto: a shorter 'restricted' shot of espresso. Made using the same dose and brew time as for a regular espresso, but with less water. The result is a richer and more intense beverage.

Roast: the process by which green coffee is heated in order to produce coffee beans ready for consumption.

Coffee Glossary contd.

Caramelisation occurs as intense heat converts starches in the bean to simple sugars, imbuing the bean with flavour and transforming its colour to a golden brown.

Robusta, Coffea canephora: the second most widely cultivated coffee species after arabica, robusta accounts for approximately 30% of the world's coffee. Robusta is hardier and grown at lower altitudes than arabica. It has a much higher caffeine content than arabica, and a less refined flavour. Commonly used in instant coffee blends.

Shot: a single unit of brewed espresso.

Single origin, single estate: coffee from one particular region or farm.

Siphon brewer, vacuum brewer: an unusual brewing method that relies on the action of a vacuum to draw hot water through coffee from one glass chamber to another. The resulting brew is remarkably clean.

Small batch: refers to roasting beans in small quantities, typically between 4-24kg, but sometimes larger.

Speciality coffee: a premium quality coffee scoring 80 points or above (from a total of 100) in the SCAA grading scale.

Steam wand: the protruding pipe found on an espresso machine that supplies hot steam used to froth and steam milk.

Stovetop, moka pot: a brewing method that makes strong coffee (but not espresso). Placed directly on a heat source, hot water is forced by steam pressure from the lower chamber to the upper chamber, passing through a bed of coffee.

Tamp: the process of distributing and pressing ground coffee into a compact bed within the portafilter basket in preparation for brewing espresso. The degree of pressure applied during tamping is a key variable in espresso extraction. Too light and the brew water will percolate rapidly (tending to under extract), too firm and the water flow will be impeded (tending to over extract).

Tamper: the small pestle-like tool used to distribute and compact ground coffee in the filter basket.

Third wave coffee: the movement that treats coffee as an artisanal foodstuff rather than a commodity product. Quality coffee reflects its terroir, in a similar manner to wine.

Under extracted: describes coffee that has not been exposed to brew water for long enough. The resulting brew is often sour and thin-bodied.

Whole bean: coffee that has been roasted but not ground.

A-Z List of Coffee Venues

UK COFFEE WEEK
APRIL 2013
The Power of Coffee
Making a difference, one cup at a time.
The annual charitable programme UK Coffee Week™ gives back to African coffee-growing countries through the nation's biggest celebration of coffee.
TEXT UKCW13 £5 TO 70070 TO DONATE *
WWW.UKCOFFEEWEEK.COM

Coffee Map Key

West End

1. The Attendant p4 *
2. The Borough Barista p5
3. Damson Café p5 *
4. Fernandez & Wells (Somerset House) p6
5. Joe & the Juice (Regent Street) p7
6. Kaffeine p8 ◊
7. Lantana p9 ◊
8. Monmouth Coffee Company (Covent Garden) p10
9. New Row Coffee p11
10. Notes (Covent Garden) p12
11. Notes (Trafalgar Square) p13 * ◊
12. The Providores and Tapa Room p14
13. Store Street Espresso p15 ◊
14. TAP Coffee (Rathbone Place) p16
15. TAP Coffee (Tottenham Court Road) p17
16. Taylor St Baristas (Mayfair) p18 * ◊
17. Workshop Coffee Co. (Marylebone) p19 ◊

Soho

18. Fernandez & Wells (Beak Street) p22 ◊
19. Flat White p23 ◊
20. Foxcroft & Ginger p24
21. Ginger & White (Soho) p25 *
22. Nude Espresso (Soho) p26
23. Princi p26
24. Rapha Cycle Club p27 * ◊
25. Sacred (Ganton Street) p28
26. Speakeasy Espresso & Brew Bar p29 ◊
27. TAP Coffee (Wardour Street) p30 * ◊

Farringdon & Clerkenwell

28. Caravan (Exmouth Market) p34
29. Department of Coffee and Social Affairs p35
30. Farm Collective (Farringdon) p36
31. Ground Control p37 *
32. Prufrock Coffee p38 ◊
33. Workshop Coffee Co. (Clerkenwell) p39 ◊

The City

34. Association Coffee p44 * ◊
35. Carter Lane Coffee p45 *
36. Chancery Coffee p45 *
37. Curators Coffee Studio p46 * ◊
38. Dose Espresso p47 ◊
39. The Fleet Street Press p48
40. The Liberty of Norton Folgate p49 *
41. Taylor St Baristas (Bank) p50

Camden & Islington

42. Bea's of Bloomsbury (Theobald's Road) p54
43. Caravan (King's Cross) p55 * ◊
44. Coffee Circus (Crouch End) p56
45. The Coffee Works Project p57 * ◊
46. The Espresso Room p58 ◊
47. The Fields Beneath p59 *
48. Fix p60
49. Free State Coffee p60 *
50. Ginger & White (Belsize Park) * p61
51. Ginger & White (Hampstead) p62
52. Harris + Hoole (Crouch End) p62 *
53. Kipferl p63
54. Leyas p63
55. Look Mum No Hands! p64 ◊
56. Maison d'Etre Coffee House p65
57. Melrose and Morgan (Primrose Hill) p65
58. Ottolenghi (Islington) p66
59. Salt p66 *
60. Timberyard p67 *

Inner East

61. Tinderbox (N1 Centre) p68
62. Vagabond (Stroud Green Road) p69 *
63. Wild & Wood Coffee p69

64. Allpress Espresso Roastery p84 ◊
65. Brick Lane Coffee p85
66. Exmouth Coffee Company p85 *
67. Fix 126 p86
68. Full Stop p87
69. Leila's p87
70. Nude Espresso (Hanbury Street) p88 ◊
71. Nude Espresso Roastery p89 *
72. Ozone Coffee Roasters p90 * ◊
73. Protein by DunneFrankowski p91 * ◊
74. Salvation Jane p92 * ◊
75. Shoreditch Grind p93
76. White Mullberries p93 *

Hackney

77. 46b Espresso Hut p96 *
78. Cà Phê VN (Saigon Street Cafe) p97
79. Climpson & Sons p98 ◊
80. Cooper & Wolf p99 *
81. The Counter Café p99
82. E5 Bakehouse p100
83. Embassy East p100 *
84. Fabrica 584 p101
85. Fred & Fran p102
86. Grind Coffee Bar (Westfield Stratford City) p102
87. The Hackney Pearl p103
88. Haggerston Espresso Room p103 *
89. Mouse & De Lotz p104
90. Railroad p105
91. Reilly Rocket p106
92. Tina, We Salute You p107
93. Wilton Way Café p108

South East

94. Arlo & Moe p112 *
95. Browns of Brockley p113 ◊
96. Café Viva p114 *
97. The Deptford Project p115
98. Fee & Brown p115 *
99. Monmouth Coffee Company (The Borough) p116 ◊
100. No67 at South London Gallery p117 *
101. ScooterCaffè p118
102. St. David Coffee House p119
103. Taylor St Baristas (Canary Wharf) p119
104. Volcano Coffee House p120 * ◊
105. With Jam and Bread p121 *

South West

106. Artisan (Putney) p124
107. Birdhouse p125
108. The Black Lab Coffee House p126
109. Brew (Clapham) p127
110. Federation Coffee p128 ◊
111. Grind Coffee Bar (Putney) p129
112. M1lk p130 *
113. The Roastery p131
114. Tried & True p131 *

West

115. Artisan (Stamford Brook) p134 *
116. Barossa p135
117. Electric Coffee Co. p136 *
118. Fernandez & Wells (South Kensington) p137 *
119. Loft Coffee Company p137 *
120. Tomtom Coffee House p138

Carts & Kiosks

A. Bean About Town * p72
B. Blooming Good Coffee p73 *
C. Coleman Coffee p73
D. Craft Coffee p74 *
E. Dark Fluid p74

F. Flat Cap Coffee Co. p75
G. Giddy Up p75
H. Merito Coffee p76
I. Pitch 42 p76
J. Terrone & Co. p77 *

* NEW
◊ TOP 30

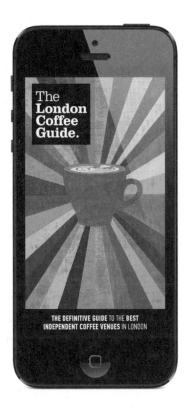